ETCHED GLASS

Techniques & Designs

This book is dedicated to the memory of our mothers,
Naomi Dobbins and Lieselotte Gabriel.

ETCHED GLASS
Techniques & Designs

Norm and Ruth Dobbins

Hand Books Press
MADISON, WISCONSIN U.S.A.

Distributed by North Light Books
CINCINNATI, OHIO U.S.A.

ETCHED GLASS
Techniques & Designs
By Norm and Ruth Dobbins

Photographer (demonstration photos): Carolyn Wright
Design: Jane Tenenbaum
Editor: Katie Kazan
Editorial Assistants: Sarah Mollet, Jennifer Thelen

©1998 by Hand Books Press

Published by
Hand Books Press, a joint venture of
THE GUILD and Design Books International
931 E. Main Street #106
Madison, WI 53703   USA
TEL 608-256-1990   TEL 800-969-1556   FAX 608-256-1938

Distributed by
North Light Books, an imprint of F&W Publications, Inc.
1507 Dana Avenue   Cincinnati, OH 45207
TEL 513-531-2222   TEL 800-289-0963

Printed in Hong Kong

ISBN 0-9658248-1-0

Title page artwork: Bonnie Brown, *Maggie Magnolia*, carved glass panel with gold leaf and limestone, 18" x 30", photo: Mel Schockner.

Front cover artwork: (top, left to right) Tohru Okamura, *Aroma*, crystal vase; Joan Irving, perfume bottle, photo: Ken West; Bonnie Brown, panel, photo: Ken Altshuler; (center,) Michael K. Hansen and Nina Paladino Caron, *California Classic Collection: Triangle*, ginger vase; (bottom) Laurie Thal and Melissa Malm, *Cobalt-Ruby Lotus* (detail), vase.

Back cover artwork: Barry Hood, *Winterwalk*, entryway, 111" x 85", photo: Roger Wade.

Ellen Abbott and Marc Leva, *Winter*, 18" x 18".

Acknowledgments

We would like to thank all the artists who were willing to share their work with us and with you, the reader. Special thanks to the staff of the Glass Art Society; Uta Klotz, the editor-in-chief of *Neues Glass*; Virginia Wright at the Corning Museum; and Kathie Edelson of Steuben Glass. Thanks also to Carolyn Wright, our photographer, who was driven to exasperation more than once by our uncooperative media, but never gave up. And a big thanks to Katie Kazan at Hand Books Press not only for her superb editing and quick grasp of things, but also for her patience with us and our ever-so-busy schedule.

Ruth and Norm Dobbins
New Mexico, March 1998

Contents

Kathy Barnard, three details from *The Sacred Grove*, carved and shaded glass wall, Reorganized Church of Latter Day Saints, Independence, MO, 15' x 12'.

Introduction

Glass has held a special fascination for man ever since the discovery, thousands of years ago, that volcanic glass—obsidian—could be made into arrowheads. From this ancient beginning, man has worked with glass in both its cooled, solid state and in its molten state. Glass has now been crafted into objects, both useful and beautiful, for more than thirty centuries. During that time period, many techniques evolved to create and manipulate glass, including the family of techniques called 'abrasive blasting.' Since the invention of the sandblaster about a hundred years ago, abrasive blasting has been used to etch and carve glass. Slow to be developed as an artistic technique or to gain widespread popularity, abrasive glass etching has blossomed in the past few years.

This is the first full-color book to be published on the techniques of abrasive glass etching, and we have written it with two primary objectives in mind. First, we wanted to satisfy the need for a thorough book of basic instruction for those would-be glass etchers who have searched and found little available on the subject. Second, we wanted to provide gallery owners, architects, interior designers, art glass collectors and all others who appreciate glass art the opportunity to understand the techniques and to appreciate the beautiful work that can be created by using them.

To this end, we have provided thorough explanations of techniques, sample projects and step-by-step photo sequences. Just as important, we have included photos of finished works from exceptional glass artists working in the United States and other countries. If you love the elegance and beauty of these works and are interested in owning pieces by the artists, we encourage you to contact them. If you want to learn how to etch glass yourself, you will find enough information here to get started and to challenge you with new techniques for a long time to come.

The instruction offered here is organized in progression starting with the easiest and simplest techniques. We have included information on designs, materials and equipment, as well as safety considerations. For those readers who want to try glass etching without renting or purchasing blasting equipment, there's information on a quick and easy form of chemical etching.

Glass etching can be an exciting hobby or a profitable career. All you need is curiosity, persistence and a willingness to experiment and have fun. Good luck in your endeavor! We hope you get as much enjoyment and satisfaction out of glass etching as we have.

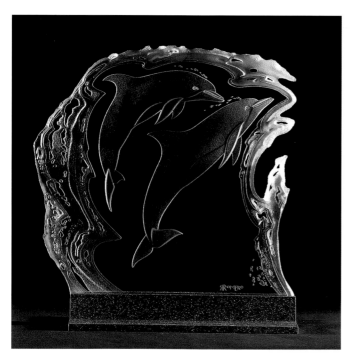

Ramon Romero, *Duet*, carved and shaded ½" plate glass, 17½"W x 18½"H x 5½"D, photo: Curt Clayton.

Author's Note

It was not easy to learn abrasive glass etching 25 years ago. There were no classes, no books, and people who knew the techniques were notorious for slamming the door (literally) in the face of anyone who dared ask how it was done. We were forced to attend the University of Experience and the School of Hard Knocks for a very long time before the secrets began to reveal themselves through the Trial and Error method of study.

We gradually became part of a network of glass artists willing to share knowledge about etching. We treasured every morsel of information gleaned, whether from our own experiments or those of others. We built or adapted our own equipment for working on glass, because there were no suppliers of such equipment. As a result, we found ourselves operating not only a glass etching studio, but also a glass etching equipment business—the first of its type in the United States.

From the beginning, we were determined to share information, writing articles and books, teaching seminars and creating instructional videos about etching. In doing so, we have discovered an age-old principle: that in teaching others, you are taught yourself. It has been fascinating to discover that we have learned as much from our students and apprentices as we have taught them.

The techniques you'll find in this book are a result of our 25 years of learning and teaching. We hope the book saves you much time getting started and being successful in etching. We also hope you enjoy the photos of the beautiful glass artwork included in this volume. This is the first published collection we know of that exclusively features etched glass art. We only ask that you respect the copyrights of the artists who have been willing to share their work here, and resist any temptation you may have to copy individual pieces.

Because the subject of abrasive glass etching is so broad and this book has a finite amount of space,

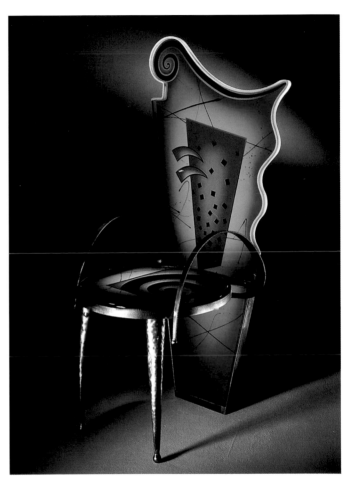

Joan Irving, *Tertiary*, chair of cut and polished ¾" plate glass and metal, etched and painted, 48"H x 20"W x 20"D, photo: Ken West.

we've had to limit what we could present here. There are many subjects, including advanced blasting techniques, coloring and gold-leafing, that we will have to cover in future books. If you just can't wait, we invite you to visit our Web site or contact us (see 'Suppliers' in the Appendices) to request our mailings.

Basics and Background

1

Glass etching is one of a family of techniques used after the initial manufacturing process to create designs on glass. Lumped under the broad category of 'glass decorating,' these techniques include hot working the glass (using a kiln to fire on paints, enamels, stains or metallic surface decoration), as well as cold-working processes that produce a design or texture by eroding the surface of the glass.

The term 'etching' usually refers to the action of an acid on a substrate, where the acid erodes the surface of the substrate. Through common usage, when applied to the decoration of a glass surface, etching has come to mean the effect of any process that erodes the glass surface to produce a frosted appearance.

Besides the use of acid, there are a number of processes that accomplish this. These include abrasive etching, wheel engraving, diamond-point or impact engraving, and laser engraving. Each produces distinctive visual effects on the glass surface that more or less resemble the effect of acid etching. These processes are commonly grouped under the general heading of 'etching,' a label that is technically inaccurate, but nonetheless pervasive.

All of these techniques can be used to produce beautiful glass art, but most have significant limitations. The primary focus of this book—abrasive etching—is by far the most versatile technique. It also has the fewest limitations and the greatest appeal, making it the method of choice for most glass-etching artists and commercial etching companies.

We also describe the use of etching cream, an easy and inexpensive approach to glass etching. Many accomplished glass-etching artists started with etching cream before moving on to abrasive etching or other techniques.

Abrasive Etching

Simply put, abrasive glass etching is the process of abrading or eroding a glass surface in selected areas through the impact of abrasive particles propelled at a high speed. The design is controlled by exposing some areas of the glass to the blast of the abrasive stream while protecting other areas with a resist material. Areas protected by the resist remain clear and unaffected by the abrasive, while exposed areas become etched. Etched glass appears translucent, white and frosted; unetched glass appears smooth, clear and dark by comparison.

Abrasive glass etching has many advantages and few drawbacks. It

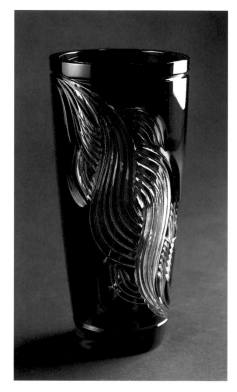

Rimpler Glass, blown flashed-glass vase, stone-wheel engraved and polished, 6"Dia x 13"H. This piece shows the characteristic V-groove shape of the wheel-engraved lines, as well as the color change that occurs in cut flashed glass.

is the only process that allows you to etch both very large areas and very fine detail quickly and accurately. It lets you etch lightly on the surface, carve deeply into the glass, or cut all the way through to

Barry Hood, *Winterwalk*, entryway, imagery created by 'shading,' an abrasive-etching technique, 111" x 85", photo: Roger Wade.

Cold-Working Techniques for Decorating Glass

	ADVANTAGES	DISADVANTAGES
Abrasive etching (also called 'abrasive blasting')	Easy to learn. Wide variety of effects. Challenging techniques at all levels of expertise. Can be used with very large or very small pieces of glass. Etches large and small areas evenly. Effective with production-line and one-of-a-kind pieces. Safe. Equipment can also be used on stone, ceramic, metal, wood.	Few classes or training materials available. Some specialized equipment necessary, although much or all can be rented.
Surface etching*	Fast method of producing graphic images of any size on any type of glass.	
Carving*	Highly controllable method for carving deep, complex images in multiple depths, as well as full-relief sculpting in thick glass.	
Shading*	Highly controllable method of creating complex images using variable gray tones (from black to white). Produces a very delicate look, similar to airbrushing.	
Chemical etching *Hydrofluoric acid*	Can produce several visual tones. Can carve deeply into the glass.	Very dangerous. Requires extensive training and special equipment. Acid is classified as hazardous waste, making disposal difficult.
*Etching cream***	Easy to learn. No special equipment required. Safe, inexpensive, readily available. Some brands suitable for production work; some environmentally friendly.	Can be used only for surface etching effects, no carving or shading. Somewhat difficult to achieve an even etch on large areas. Etch is visually 'flat' compared to abrasive etch.
Wheel engraving *Copper wheel*	Can produce beautifully detailed designs. Can carve into the glass.	Unsuitable for engraving large areas or large pieces of glass. Except in Europe, instruction is very hard to find. Requires a fairly long learning curve. Equipment difficult to locate.
Stone wheel	Produces coarse to moderately detailed V-shaped and U-shaped grooved engraving. Polished grooves (called 'brilliant cutting') give a beautiful finish on cut (stone-wheel engraved) crystal pieces.	Unsuitable for large areas or pieces of glass. Except in Europe, instruction is very hard to find. Requires a fairly long learning curve. Equipment is difficult to locate.
Diamond-point engraving	Inexpensive, hand-held diamond-point scribe is the only tool you need.	Effects are limited to scratched lines. Unsuitable for etching large areas or for carving. Shading limited to cross hatching. Slow.
Impact engraving	Inexpensive, hand-held vibrating engraver with carbide or diamond point. Can be used on materials other than glass.	Effects limited to dots and lines. Unsuitable for etching large areas or for carving. Shading limited to cross hatching, stippling. Slow.
Rotary engraving	Hand-held rotary grinder, either electric (inexpensive) or air-powered (more expensive), uses diamond or carbide burrs. Relatively easy to use. Works well for line drawings and signatures. Can carve into glass. Can be used on other materials.	Effects limited to dots and lines. Unsuitable for carving. Unsuitable when an even etch of large areas is needed. Shading limited to cross hatching and stippling. Slow.
Laser engraving	Computer driven. No hand work necessary. Easy to repeat designs. Equipment can be used with other materials.	Very expensive equipment. Effects limited to surface etch. Tiny areas of heat stress cause etched areas to 'flake' for months or years.

*These techniques are described in detail in this book.

actually shape the glass. It can be used to create any style of artwork at any level of complexity, and it can be used with any size piece of glass. It's easy to learn, challenging, and very safe when common precautions are taken.

Until recently, abrasive blasting was more commonly called 'sandblasting.' That term is fading out of use because sand is seldom used for blasting today. Newer abrasives have become available recently that are harder, sharper, longer lasting and safer to use.

THREE VERY DIFFERENT EFFECTS

The three primary abrasive-etching techniques—surface etching, carving and shading—are distinguished from each other by the extent of blasting received by the glass, and by whether the blasting is accomplished in one stage or more. The same design will look very different when surface etched than when carved or shaded, and as you'll see in the artwork shown throughout this book, some very effective designs use combinations of the three techniques.

Other factors influence the appearance of the etching as well. The texture (or fineness) of the surface is controlled by the size of the abrasive particles. Two factors—blasting time and air pressure—determine the depth of carving and degree of shading.

Because it's attractive and low in cost, surface etching is the most commonly used of these techniques. It's the first abrasive etching technique learned by novices, and—since production time is short—the most viable commercial technique. However, surface etching is simply not as expressive as shading and carving, and most of the surface-etched artwork shown in this book also utilizes the other techniques.

Norm and Ruth Dobbins, demonstration project showing the three main etching techniques. The mask on the left is surface etched, showing high contrast and a flat graphic appearance. The center mask is multistage carved; it shows three-dimensional contour carving and appears white-on-white. The mask on the right is multistage shaded, and features variable gray tones that create a dramatic, three-dimensional appearance, even though the etching is only on the glass surface.

STAGED BLASTING

A major reason that carving and shading are so expressive is that they're multistage techniques. By blasting in multiple stages, the artist can create a more realistic and sophisticated design.

How is this accomplished? Well, consider surface etching, which is a single-stage technique. Because the blasting is done all at once—and all elements are etched to 100 percent white—the only way edges of individual elements can be distinguished from each other is by separating them with a clear space. In other words, where one etched flower petal touches another, there would be no way to tell where one

Abrasive Etching Techniques	
Surface Etching	Exposed areas of the design are blasted to a 100-percent density on the glass surface. The etching is completed in one stage.
Carving	Glass is blasted for a much longer period of time, usually at a higher pressure, so that the design areas are eroded deeply into the glass. Carving can be done in one or multiple stages.
Shading	The extent of blasting on the glass is deliberately varied from zero to 100 percent to produce apparent shades of gray in different elements of the design. Shading is usually done in multiple stages.

J.D. Francis, multistage-carved and shaded window panel (detail), private residence, 14" x 24".

The sequence of the stages is very important. When etched in the correct sequence, the finished piece *looks* right and is true to the design. For this reason, a large part of learning carving and shading techniques is learning how to determine the correct sequence for etching the elements of the design. In fact, this is one of two major considerations in learning either multistage technique. Analyzing the design for the proper sequence of blasting is a thought process that relies on the artist's understanding of both the design and the chosen blasting technique, in relation to each other.

The second major consideration with multistage blasting is the ability to physically create the desired effect with the blasting equipment. This comes from practice, and nothing else.

Each abrasive-etching technique has its own visual strengths and weaknesses. With a good understanding of these qualities, the etching artist can combine techniques in the best possible way The ultimate accomplishment of a glass etching artist is to have an equally good understanding and command of each technique as well as the ability to combine them effectively.

Etching Cream

This book also describes the use of etching cream, a safe, easy and inexpensive way to get started in glass etching. This technique gives good results, especially with smaller projects like glassware and gift items.

The element that erodes glass in both hydrofluoric acid and etching cream is fluorine. In etching cream, the fluorine is within a relatively safe chemical compound called bifluoride. In addition to be-

stops and the other starts unless they are separated by a narrow clear space. As a result, designs which are surface etched tend to be simple and unrealistic, though often very appealing.

Now, if you blast in multiple stages, you can create the distinctions between elements in a more realistic way. With carving, distinctions are created by blasting ele-

ments to different depths where they touch each other. With shading, the distinction is made by etching elements to a different shade of gray where they touch. In both cases, the resist is removed from different elements of the design at sequential stages in the blasting process, thereby achieving the desired depth of carving or degree of shading on each element.

Barry Sautner, *Deciduous Desires*, abrasive-carved high-relief blown glass, 7⅝"H x 3¾"Dia.

ing safer than hydrofluoric acid, etching cream differs in that it etches only the glass surface, as opposed to eroding deeply into the glass. It also leaves a more frosted finish, while the surface left by hydrofluoric acid is nearly clear.

There are several manufacturers of etching creams. Each product has slightly different application procedures. While some are reusable, others are not. Some are more environmentally friendly than others. Each gives slightly different results.

Whether you'll be etching by abrasive blasting or with etching cream, the preparation is the same; only the actual method of producing the etched surface differs. Thus, time spent learning to resize and transfer designs or select and

Ellen Abbott and Mark Leva, surface-etched, multistage-carved and shaded panel with appliquéd colored glass jewels and other colored glass elements, 32" x 66".

Barbara Boeck, multistage-carved wall inset of ½" plate glass (detail), edge lit, 18" x 56" overall. Edge lighting is a dramatic way to show off a design carved on flat glass.

apply resists will be well worthwhile, whether or not you eventually move from etching cream to abrasive etching.

What Can You Etch?

The easy answer to this question is, "Just about anything made of glass." Although the current interest in etching grows out of the renaissance in architectural stained glass, the use of etching has developed far beyond that application. Glass etching is now used in at least six major areas of commercial and artistic endeavor.

Decorative architectural glasswork in commercial and residential buildings and churches, including

Don Young, detail of a 500-square-foot window wall installation for the J. Erik Jonsson Central Library Children's Center, Dallas, TX. Photo stencil halftone etching in combination with surface etching.

Margaret Oldman, *Sun Princess*, multistage-carved and shaded three-panel screen, 61" x 61", collection of the Imperial Palace, Tokyo. The gray areas, produced by the shading technique, give a welcome change of contrast from the white, carved elements, and help to emphasize them.

Eric W. Bergman, surface-etched tabletop.

windows, doors, privacy screens, room partitions, window walls and commemorative glass walls.

Commercial, residential and marine interior design, including glass tabletops, fireplace screens, folding room dividers, stairway railings, restaurant booth dividers, mirrors, lighting fixtures, shower and bath enclosures, and interior glass partitions and walls in air-ports, commercial and professional buildings, homes and yachts.

Signage, including interior glass signs in hotels, restaurants, office buildings and malls.

Awards and recognition pieces, including corporate presentation pieces, glass awards, commemoratives and plaques.

Gifts, both corporate and personal, including paperweights, nameplates, decanters, wine glasses, beer mugs, vases, bowls, glass boxes, bookends, bottles, wine bottles (unopened, with wine inside!) and much more.

Works of art, both functional and nonfunctional, sculptures and two-dimensional or curved panels.

Over the years, our students have etched everything from watch crystals and eyeglass lenses, to television picture tubes (an art project), to large wall partitions. One student was so enthralled with etching that she decorated practically every piece of glass in her house, including the glass shelves in the bathroom medicine cabinet.

Workspace Requirements

Although a workbench is ideal, you can work comfortably with etching cream—or to prepare small projects for abrasive etching—at the kitchen table. You'll need to protect the table surface from being scratched by the glass or discolored by the cream. Cover the table with a sheet of plastic or inexpensive plastic tablecloth. A piece of masonite, homosote or plywood placed over the plastic will protect the table as you cut your resist. Follow the manufacturer's instructions carefully as you apply and wash off the etching cream; some brands will etch the finish of a porcelain sink or discolor stainless steel.

For abrasive etching, you'll also need space for equipment: an air compressor, blaster and blasting cabinet. Although these can vary considerably in size, a standard setup—one that will handle sheets of glass up to 2' x 4'—will take up about the same amount of space as a refrigerator, washer and dryer. Other than the equipment and abrasive, no special tools or supplies are required. You will need a

Sample project by the authors illustrates the difference in appearance of abrasive etching (whiter areas) and etching cream (grayer areas). The two techniques can be used together, as here, to produce a two-toned surface etching.

David Stone, *Lady & Landscape*, fireplace screen, surface-etched and multistage-carved and shaded ½" plate glass on steel base.

stencil knife, ruler and squeegee, and some self-adhesive vinyl or rubber resist, all available locally or through mail-order suppliers.

Getting Started

Sample projects beginning in Chapter 5 illustrate the principles of each etching technique and give you a hands-on foundation for which there is no substitute. Project patterns are included in the Appendix; feel free to use them for your personal projects. Permission is required for commercial use of the patterns.

Your next step? Get started! Glass etching is a wonderfully satisfying process that yields beautiful results. There's also a lot of fun in the bargain, so don't wait to begin.

Margaret Oldman, *Clift Palace*, flat glass, slumped into a bowl shape, with multistage-carved design and edge shaped by abrasive blasting, 20"Dia.

2

A Glass Primer

Glass is a material unlike any other in the world. It is hard, strong, brittle and smooth. It reflects light at certain angles; at others, light passes straight through it. Perhaps its most amazing characteristic is that—in its purest form—it is invisible. Although most glass has chemical additives or colorants that render it visible, the only way you can see a clean piece of optically clear glass is by the light reflected from its surface.

When clear glass is etched, the design becomes visible against the background of the 'invisible' unetched surface. The image appears to float in midair. It somehow seems like magic.

Glass is available in innumerable shapes, forms and colors, and hundreds of different chemical compositions. To explore the many possibilities offered by glass etching, you need to understand the unique qualities of some common types of glass. Armed with this knowledge, you'll make wise choices about which glass to use for any particular project.

When choosing glass, pay attention to both its chemical composition and its physical attributes, including form, thickness-to-size ratio, color, texture, and special treatments and functions (mirror, safety glass, etc.). These characteristics

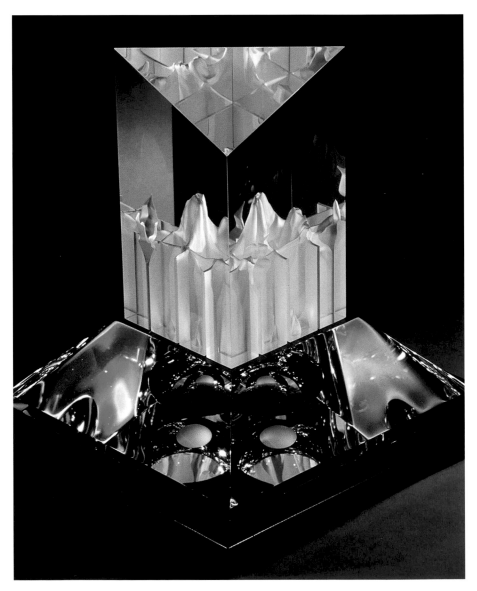

Eric Hilton, *Time's Flow*, optical crystal, cut, carved and polished, on a stained wood base, private collection, 14"H x 10"W x 10"D.

Elizabeth Mears, *Days of Creation*, menorah, lampworked borosilicate glass with abrasive-etched elements.

affect the type of etching that can be done on a particular piece of glass, and how the finished piece will look.

The Basic Recipe

The main component of glass is silicon dioxide—which you may know better as silica sand, the kind used in sand boxes and concrete. Other chemicals and fluxing agents are added to emphasize certain characteristics of the glass. These chemicals affect hardness, heat resistance, clarity, color and other characteristics that are important to specific applications.

At about 2,000°F, these ingredients melt and become liquid. The glass can then be formed into finished products through 'hot' manufacturing processes. It can be rolled or drawn, or a thin layer can be floated on a bed of molten tin to make flat sheets; it can also be cast, pressed or blown into three-dimensional pieces. Once it's formed and cooled, glass can be further altered and refined by cutting, sawing, grinding, polishing and etching. These are called 'cold' processes.

Initially, all glass is *annealed* during manufacturing. This means it is cooled in a slow, controlled process that minimizes stress in the glass. Annealing makes it possible to work with the glass using

Ruth Dobbins, left: crystal vase, single stage carved, 7" x 13"; right: soda lime candy bowl, surface etched, 11" x 12", photo: Carolyn Wright.

cold processes, with a low probability of it shattering from internal stress.

The most common glass is *soda lime* glass, named for two of its key chemical constituents. This type of glass is used in making most flat sheets—including window glass and plate glass—and much of the glass tableware used today. This glass is readily available, low in cost, and easy to etch.

BOROSILICATE GLASS

Glass containers that will be subjected to great changes in temperature, including casseroles and other cookware, are made of *borosilicate* glass. This type of glass is characterized by its hardness and resistance to cracking when exposed to high heat. It's seldom used in etching, primarily because the baking dishes, measuring cups and other objects made from it are not generally viewed as decorative objects. Pyrex is a brand name for one variation of borosilicate glass.

Borosilicate glass is also used in *lampworking*, the type of glass blowing in which artists use a torch to create figurines and sculptures. Glass blowers sometimes etch the glass after the figures are created. Because of its hardness, borosilicate takes a bit longer to etch than soda lime glass. Some etching creams do not work on borosilicate.

LEAD CRYSTAL

Lead crystal glass is made by adding lead oxide to the glass mixture. Lead crystal is renowned for its brilliant clarity, its high refractive index and its softness, which makes it easy to cut and polish. Because the term 'lead crystal' is often shortened to simply 'crystal,' people sometimes think this glass is actually quartz or some other type of mineral crystal—a complete misconception.

Lead crystal is usually considered the most beautiful type of glass, and it is the most expensive of the commonly available glasses. It is used almost exclusively in high-end glassware like wine goblets, carafes and decanters, vases and bowls. It's also the glass used for the cut-crystal glassware found in fine gift shops and some jewelry stores, as well as the decorative prisms used in chandeliers, crystal jewelry, and window ornaments. Lead crystal etches easily, but it also scratches easily. Handle it carefully.

There are more than 300 varieties of crystal glass, including some—only recently available on the mass market—that do not contain lead. These may eventually replace lead crystal because of the health concerns surrounding the use of lead in products used with food.

Most other types of specialty glass are so unusual and expensive that they're rarely considered for etching. These include optical glass and glass for military applications. One specialty glass, a combination of glass and ceramic, can take extreme heat without cracking or melting, and is used to make heat tiles on the space shuttle. The only place you're likely to run into this type of glass here on Earth (where it *is* successfully etched) is in the doors of modern wood stoves. These windows of ceramic and glass have now almost entirely replaced borosilicate and tempered glass in wood stoves.

TEMPERING

The glass you use in etching projects will almost always be annealed. The one exception is *tem-*

pered glass. Tempering is the process of reheating glass after manufacture, and then cooling it in a very fast, precise process. This process creates controlled stress in the glass (as opposed to random and uneven stress, which sometimes occurs when glass is cooled too rapidly during the annealing process). The controlled stress of tempering is used to strengthen the glass and/or make it function as safety glass.

It's important to know when you're using tempered glass, since it can't be etched in all the ways annealed glass can. See more about tempered glass in the section on safety glass, later in this chapter.

Physical Characteristics

The physical attributes of glass are very important in glass etching. To understand these attributes is to understand not only the limitations they place on the glass etcher, but also the full range of possibilities they offer.

FLAT GLASS

Flat (or sheet) glass is the glass that windows are made of. It's also used to make door panels, tabletops, shelves and display units, partitions, room dividers, bath enclosures, mirrors, ornaments and many other products.

Both window glass (which is $1/8$" thick) and plate glass ($1/4$" thick or more) are sometimes called *float* glass because of the manufacturing process of 'floating' the glass on a bed of molten tin to make it perfectly flat. Most float glass is clear, but it is also available in a few colors. Stained glass, which is available in thousands of colors, is flat glass that is made with a rolling process (although some stained glass is still hand blown into cylin-

Jean-Paul Raymond, *Jour D'Été*, etched and carved optical crystal with gold leaf, $17\frac{3}{4}$" x $17\frac{3}{4}$".

Barbara Boeck, curved, laminated glass wall inset with edge lighting, 48" x 60" x $1/2$". Laminated plate glass, bent to conform to the curve of the wall. Multistage carving and shading techniques are used together in this piece.

Common Flat Glass Stock

COMMON NAME	THICKNESS	USE
Window glass		
Single strength	3/32" (2 mm)	Once the standard for windows, but seldom used for this purpose anymore. Too thin for most kinds of etching.
Double strength	1/8" (3 mm)	The standard window glass, used for most surface etching and shading projects up to about five square feet. Very affordable.
Plate glass		
Standard plate	3/16" (5 mm) or 1/4" (6 mm)	3/16" plate can be used for surface etching projects up to about 10 square feet. 1/4" plate is commonly used for surface etching projects up to 4' x 8' and for carved projects up to about 3' x 8'.
Heavy plate	3/8", 1/2", and 3/4" (9 mm, 12 mm, and 18 mm)	Also called 'heavy glass.' Most often used for large carved projects or smaller projects where the carving is very deep. Edge polishing is important for exposed edges (and adds to the cost).
Mirror	1/8" (3 mm) and 1/4" (6 mm)	Window or 1/4" plate glass with a mirrored backing.
Safety glass		
Laminated	Thickness varies	Two sheets of thin glass bonded into one thicker sheet. Most commonly 1/8" bonded to 1/8" to make a 1/4" sheet, but also available in thicker versions.
Tempered	Thickness varies	Flat glass of any thickness which has been deliberately heat stressed so that it breaks into small fragments when struck.
Stained glass	1/8"	Colored and/or textured glass sold through stained glass suppliers.

ders, then split lengthwise and flattened). Rolling doesn't produce sheets as flat and smooth as the float process, but it gives the glass great character.

In most cases, plate glass factories make flat glass in large sheets, up to 10' x 17'. Stained glass is made in sheets of many different sizes, with the largest about 2 1/2' x 7' and the average size about 2' x 4'.

Sheets of both plate and stained glass are sold to manufacturers who use them in many kinds of products. Plate glass companies cut glass for both standard and custom-sized windows for installation into commercial buildings and homes.

Glass tabletop manufacturers cut heavy glass into large pieces for tables and shelving. Still others cut 1/4" plate glass into standard sizes and shapes, then bevel and polish the edges for use in leaded beveled windows, lamps and chandeliers. Glass awards, corporate recognition pieces and desk accessories are made from heavy glass that is cut into small pieces and highly polished at the edges. Stained glass businesses, of course, use glass in windows, lampshades and other decorative and gift items. All of these products are made from flat glass and all are candidates for etching.

For most projects calling for flat glass, you'll probably use 1/8" or 1/4" window glass or mirror. Because these types of glass are clear and colorless, they show off etching very well. They can be purchased at a stained glass supply shop or plate glass shop, whichever is more convenient and carries the size you need. Quarter-inch plate glass with beveled edges (usually just called *beveled* glass) gives an elegant look to any etching. Heavy glass (3/8" to 3/4") shows off carving better than any other option, but is harder to find and considerably more expensive.

For large architectural pieces

you will need to contact a plate glass shop; stained glass suppliers rarely carry large sizes because of space limitations and safety concerns.

Size-to-Thickness Ratio

Size should never be the only determining factor when choosing glass for etching projects. When working with flat glass, you should always consider the thickness of the glass compared to the size of the piece. The larger the glass, the thicker it should be to withstand pressure on the surface (e.g., wind on a window or someone pushing on a door panel). Generally, double-strength glass is safe to use in sizes up to about five square feet; any project larger than that should be made with at least 1/4" plate glass. Keep in mind that etching will weaken the surface of the glass, so always go for thicker stock if you have any question.

When determining thickness, it's also important to consider the etching techniques to be used. With surface etching or shading projects up to five square feet, 1/8" window glass will be adequate. For larger surface etching and shading projects—up to 4' x 8'—use 1/4" plate glass or safety glass as required by building codes for specific applications. When carving, you'll always want to use at least 1/4" plate glass. If you're not sure what thickness to use for a given project, consult a plate glass supplier or glazing contractor.

Edge Finish

Edge finish is an important consideration in etching projects made with flat glass and exposed edges. The cost of edge finish is not prohibitive and the perceived value of a piece will be much higher if the edges are beautifully polished. There are a number of different types of edge finishes, including

Wally Zampa, *Poseidon*, surface-etched, tempered 1/2" glass doors and transom for a shower enclosure, photo: Ed Asmus.

beveling (where the edge is ground and polished at an angle to the surface), *pencil polish* (rounded edge) and *flat polish* (flat edge). Several variations appear on the next page.

Pieces of plate glass with beveled edges are available from stained glass suppliers in sizes up to about 6" x 9". These pieces are sold for making leaded beveled windows, but they make great ornaments or table decorations when

etched. Larger pieces of beveled plate glass (available by custom order) are beautiful when etched and installed in windows or doors. Beveled mirrors provide much nicer finished projects than plain mirrors. If you are etching a glass tabletop, frameless shower door, glass shelf or any other project using heavy glass with exposed edges, the edges should be polished, both for looks and safety.

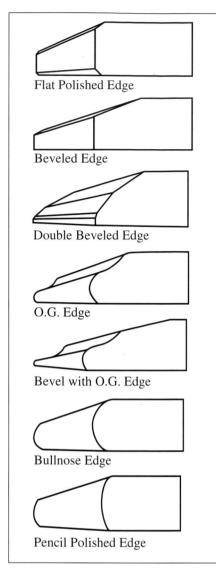

Profiles of several popular edge finishes on heavy glass tabletops and glass award blanks. All edges are ground to shape, then polished.

Flat Polished Edge

Beveled Edge

Double Beveled Edge

O.G. Edge

Bevel with O.G. Edge

Bullnose Edge

Pencil Polished Edge

Joan Irving, *Fleur de Lis*, carved, abrasive-etched glass chair with reverse painting, metal frame, ³⁄₄" plate glass, custom cut and polished, 50" x 20" x 20", photo: Ken West. The etched surface provides a roughened surface or 'tooth' for the paint to adhere to. The top of the chair back has been cut and shaped with the sandblaster.

THREE-DIMENSIONAL GLASS

By 'three-dimensional' glass, we mean almost any piece of glass that is not a flat sheet. This can include flat glass that is slumped or bent (like the curved fronts of some antique cabinets); blown glass objects like vases, bowls and glassware; or thick pieces of cast glass with flat or curved surfaces.

Applying etching resist to a curved surface is more difficult than applying it to a flat surface. Transferring and cutting a design are also more difficult with three-dimensional glass. How you approach these steps will depend upon the curvature of the glass and whether you plan to etch on the front or back surface. See Chapter 4 ("Design") and Chapter 3 ("Resists") for more information.

Clear crystal glass and clear or colored soda lime glass are the most commonly etched three-dimensional glasses. Glass tableware and other three-dimensional glass items are available from discount stores, department stores, factory outlets, gift shops, glassware stores, restaurant supply companies and many other sources. Almost any glass products you find in these places can be etched. The exceptions are glass coffee mugs and other containers for hot liquids. These are sometimes tempered to add strength and make them resistant to heat cracking; if so, they should not be carved, although they can be safely surface etched or shaded. (See the discussion of tempered glass later in this chapter.)

COLOR

Most kinds of glass are available as transparent and colorless (usually

Far left:
Tohru Okamura,
Paradise, wine
cooler of soda
lime glass, surface
etched and single
stage carved,
7"Dia x 6¾".

Left: Barry Hood,
Great Northern,
arched window in
3 pieces, ¼" plate
glass, multistage
carved and shaded,
9' x 4½'.

called 'clear'), transparent and colored (usually just called 'colored'), and translucent and colored. Translucent glass (e.g., opalescent stained glass) is sometimes mistakenly called opaque, even though it passes light through. Truly opaque glass is quite unusual. Both opaque and translucent glass should be etched only on the front surface, since you can't see the etching through the glass.

Designs can be etched equally well on any of these types of glass. Since the etched design looks white, it stands out particularly well on dark glass or on clear glass placed in front of a dark background. Clear glass is etched much more often than colored simply because it is used more often in day-to-day settings.

Stained Glass

Other than with colored glassware, you're most likely to encounter color in stained glass. Your supplier can provide you with sheets of innumerable colors, which can be used for great gifts. In addition to regular clear or opalescent stained glass, unique choices like *iridized*, *dichroic* and *flashed* glass can give some wonderful special effects. Flashed glass has a thin layer of colored glass over a thicker layer of clear or light-colored glass. Etching

Michael Hansen and Nina Paladino Caron, *Erika Perfume: Twigs*, etched hand-blown perfume bottle, clear glass over black iridized, 4½"Dia x 6"H.

Laurie Thal and Melissa Malm, *Yellow Lotus*, blown flashed glass bowl, 5" x 14", etched to reveal the contrasting base glass color.

Zoe Pasternak, *Koi*, leaded stained glass window, 28"Dia. Abrasive etching on flashed glass results in the texture and color splotches on both the fish and the background. Both metal mesh and liquid resist were used.

the surface coating away in the design area gives the contrast of the base color against the coating color. This is one way to get a two-colored etching. Similarly, iridized and dichroic glass are coated on one surface with metallic-vapor deposits that reflect a myriad of different colors. Abrasive etching on the metallic side can remove the coating in selected areas, with some very interesting effects.

Since stained glass is only 1/8" thick, it can be used for surface etching and shading, but not for carving. However, plate glass—which *is* suitable for carving—can occasionally be found in colors. Check with a stained glass supplier or plate glass shop; either one may have a few colors of plate glass available.

When etching on colored glass, it's usually best to etch on the *first surface* (the side closest to the viewer), because the etching will show up better in all lighting conditions. Etching done on the *second surface* of a medium or dark piece of glass will not show up at all unless there is strong light coming through the glass. Etching on colored glass gives you two shades of the same color, in contrast to etching on flashed glass, which gives two entirely different colors.

TEXTURE

Glass with textured surfaces (like some shower-door glass and some stained glass) can be etched, but the etching does not show up as well as it does on a smooth surface. If the finished piece is mounted in front of a slightly dark background and the etching is done on the first surface, it will show up tolerably well, but it's better to start with smooth glass or glass with very little texture.

MIRRORED GLASS

Mirror is just window or plate glass with a mirror coating on one side. If you etch on the front of a piece of mirror, you'll get a double image: the etching itself and the reflection of the etching in the mirrored backing. Depending on the subject matter and complexity of the design, this effect can add depth of perspective and visual interest, or can simply look confusing. Only through experimentation and experience can you tell whether a particular design will work well etched on the front of the mirror.

For a completely different effect, you can use abrasive blasting to etch through the mirror's silver backing. Blasting etches the glass at the same time that it removes the mirror, so your design shows the contrast between the etched white surface of the glass and the silver mirror. There is no double image in this case, since the etching is on the same level as the mirror backing.

Etching creams are not effective in removing the silver backing of mirrored glass. However, a chemical backing remover is available from many hobby and craft supply shops. It can be used with a resist, very much like etching cream, but although it effectively removes the mirror, it will not etch the glass. Etching cream can be used as a second step, once the mirror remover is thoroughly cleaned from the glass and the resist.

Special Effects with Mirrors

When the mirror is mounted on a wall, the etched design looks noticeably more gray than it would if etched on the front. It also picks up the color of the wall or whatever backing is used in the frame. Similarly, if the mirror is hung in front of a window or mounted in a light

Annie Morningstar, carved wine bottles utilizing client art and logos, photo: Michael Craft Photography. The glass is carved deeply enough to hold a thick application of opaque color.

box, the etching appears much brighter and whiter, and the silver of the mirror appears darker by comparison. In this case, the overall look of the piece changes completely from day to night, or when the light is on or off.

For an easy special effect, you can airbrush or spray paint the etching on the back of the mirror. This creates a striking contrast between the mirror and the color-enhanced etching. Alternately, you can glue pieces of colored foil or glass over various areas of the etching. The color will come through

Don Young, 1/4" plate glass mirror, etched from the back with photo resist and backlit, 6' x 16'.

the translucent etched design as a muted, pastel version of the color of the backing element. If you spray the etching with clear lacquer before you attach the colored elements, the etching becomes clearer, and the color brighter.

Mirrored glass can be readily found in silver, bronze and gray colors at plate glass shops. A few other colors are available, but are more difficult to find.

SAFETY GLASS

Building codes require the use of safety glass in certain locations where people could be harmed if the glass were to break. These locations include door panels and sidelights, any window which comes within 18" of the floor, shower stalls, permanently mounted room dividers, and restaurant booth dividers, to name just a few. Check your local building codes or ask your local plate glass shop for specifics. Regulations of this type were initiated in the early 1970s, when sliding glass doors had become popular in homes. Occasionally people walked into these doors and broke the glass, with serious consequences.

Tempered Glass

The most common form of safety glass is tempered glass. This glass has been deliberately stressed by crash cooling during fabrication, causing it to be tougher than regular annealed glass. In addition, when struck hard enough to break, it explodes into thousands of small chunks, with the effect of minimizing injury from flying pieces.

Tempered glass can be surface etched and shaded, but not carved. It requires special handling, including the use of fine abrasives and low blasting pressures. Proceed as you would with annealed glass, but cut back your pressure 20 to 30

John Morrison, *Spiramid*, laminated and carved glass sculpture, 14" x 14" x 11".

Rebecca Odom, *Murphy*, trumpet vase, 11¼" x 5¾"Dia. The artist has carved a purchased crystal vase and colored it by rubbing with a "soupy mixture" of artist oils and drying media.

Elizabeth Mears, goblet with cane stem, lampworked borosilicate glass with abrasive-etched elements.

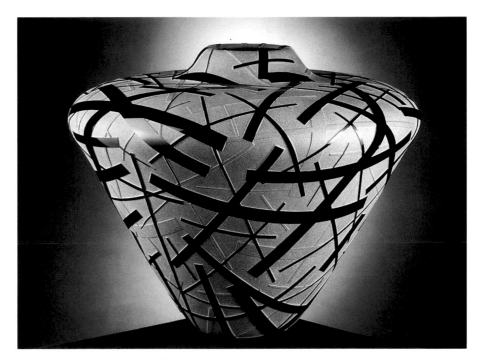

Michael Hansen and Nina Paladino Caron, ginger vase with *Sticks* pattern, surface-etched blown glass, 8" x 8".

percent, and be sure your abrasive is no larger than 120 grit. It's also important to keep your nozzle further from the surface than you would with annealed glass.

It's easy to shatter a piece of flat tempered glass by knocking an edge a little too hard while handling it, or by using too much pressure and blasting too deep. Three-dimensional tempered glass, as in coffee mugs, is quite a bit stronger. Still, we do not recommend the use of tempered glass by beginners.

Laminated Glass

The other common type of safety glass is laminated glass. Its standard form is a sandwich of two pieces of $1/8$" glass bonded by a layer of clear polyvinyl film. This creates a product $1/4$" thick which will not fall apart when broken. (The windshield of your car is made with this material.) Thicker laminated glass is available by special order.

Laminated glass can be safely surface etched or shaded, but carving is problematic. When you carve $1/4$" laminated glass, you are really carving into a sheet of $1/8$" glass. If you go more than one-third of the way through, the glass will be weakened enough to break easily, but the carving will not be sufficiently deep to show up well. If you really need to carve on laminated glass, consider ordering $1/2$" glass (made of two $1/4$" layers) or $3/8$" glass (which is made of an $1/8$" layer bonded to a $1/4$" layer). Generally, anything other than $1/4$" laminated glass must be specially made, so the cost will be substantial. In any case, laminated glass must be ordered cut to size from a plate glass shop, as it is difficult to cut without special training and experience.

CLEANING THE GLASS SURFACE

The glass surface must be clean in order for the resist material to adhere. Any spots of dirt, grease or oil (even from fingerprints) will prevent the resist from sticking. If the resist does not stick, it may lift off during the blasting process, ruining the project. The resist is particularly vulnerable to lift-off around cut areas of your design.

You can use household products to clean your glass, including vinegar, ammonia or alcohol, but commercial cleaners are much easier to use. Just read the list of ingredients, and don't use any cleaner

John Morrison, *To boldly go...*, multistage carved and surface etched custom laminated glass sculpture, with applied clear coat in the carved areas, 9"H x 5½" thick, collection of Mrs. Gene Rodenberry.

that contains silicone; it will keep the resist from sticking well. Likewise, when working with mirror, don't use ammonia or any cleaners containing ammonia; it causes a deterioration of the silver backing that basically ruins the mirror over time. You may have noticed this effect, which professional glazers call *black-edge*, on antique mirrors.

For best results on any type of glass, we recommend the glass cleaners available from stained glass suppliers and plate glass shops. These cleaners come in a spray can and expel a white foam which cleans streak-free. It takes very little of this product to do the job.

Newspaper or paper towels can be used with the cleaners, but don't use them dry. Dry paper can scratch glass—especially crystal, which is both soft and expensive compared to other glasses. It's best to use clean cloths or soft, lint-free paper towels available from cleaning supply companies. If you use cloth or paper that is not lint free, be sure to blow or brush off any lint that remains after cleaning, before applying the resist.

Glass is an exciting medium to work with—almost seductive in its beauty and magic. In our seminars, it's always gratifying to watch people's eyes light up when they finish their first etching. We'd like to believe it's because of our exciting teaching style—but we know it's really the glass.

Lucinda Shaw, *The Basilica*, ½" plate glass, surface etched, carved and polished, 15" x 13" x 12". This was a gift from the citizens of Baltimore to Pope John Paul II, and is in the Vatican collection.

3

Resist

Resist covers and protects the glass surface in areas determined by the artist, while exposing the glass to the etching process in other areas. The resist can be a sheet of self-adhesive rubber or vinyl, or a liquid that dries tough and hard on the glass. It can be a piece of wire mesh or a plastic leaf or your own hand, protected by a rubber glove. By carefully choosing and using a resist, the glass etcher controls the design of the etching on the glass—where it's placed and how it looks.

There are two basic categories of resist and many choices within each category. You need to be able to choose the best option for your particular project. Occasionally, you may even choose a combination of resist materials.

Resists Used for Glass Etching

Sheet resists
- Vinyls (hard and soft)
- Clear vinyl
- Rubber
- Photo resist
- Precut resist

Found resists
- Materials inherently resistant to etching
- Liquids
- Materials which can be treated to become resistant

Michael Hanson and Nina Paladino Caron, *Erika Perfume: Enterprise*, carved hand-blown perfume bottle, with applied gold color, 4½" x 6"H.

Sheet resists can be obtained from stained glass suppliers—either locally or by mail. See the list of suppliers in the Appendix.

Characteristics of Resist

Each type of resist has its own physical characteristics, including how thick and tough it is, how it's applied to the glass, and whether it's a solid or liquid. These variables dictate how the design is produced and the ultimate visual appearance of the etched glass. A sheet resist yields an etching with a sharp, well-defined edge; a liquid resist that wears away (intentionally) as you blast gives a softer, more organic look, with a slightly fuzzy edge.

Resists are used to create areas of etched texture, as well as designs. These can be pronounced aspects of the design, or background patterns intended to obscure the view through the glass. Look for examples of these kinds of textures in the projects shown throughout this book.

Most—but not all—resist materials used by glass etchers are made specifically for glass, and most—but not all—can be used effectively with etching cream as well as abrasive etching. Resists should be of proper thickness for the technique to be used and they should be easy to apply and remove, without leaving any residue behind on the glass. The thickness of a resist is rated in *mils* (thousandths of an inch).

Choosing a Resist

By far, the most commonly used resists are relatively thin, flat sheets of adhesive-backed vinyl or rubber. These resists come in rolls 12" to 36" wide and 10 to 50 yards long.

Primary Characteristics of Resists

Toughness
The resist needs to be tough enough to withstand the abrasive for the length of time you'll be blasting (which varies depending upon the etching technique used). The thicker a resist material is, the tougher it is. Some resists are inherently tougher than others.

Adhesive
The adhesive on the resist should hold firmly to the glass during blasting, yet release easily when you are finished, without leaving a residue.

Flexibility
The resist used on flat glass does not need to be as flexible as the resist used on three-dimensional glass.

Cost
The thicker, tougher and more flexible the resist, the more expensive it will be. Naturally, you don't want to get a heavier resist than you need. On the other hand, if you use a resist that's too thin in the name of saving money, it may release or shred during blasting, and you'll face the expense of replacing a ruined piece of glass. Resist with the best adhesive for glass is made especially for etching. It is somewhat difficult to find, but not particularly expensive.

Bonnie Brown, test piece, multistage carved with textures, 12" x 10", photo: Ken Altshuler. The background texture, created by use of a liquid resist with the shading technique, sets off the carved design in a unique and effective way.

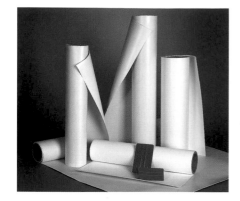

Rubber and vinyl sheet resist vary in color from white to tan to pale green. Rolls range from 12" to 36". Also shown: application squeegees in two sizes.

Other types of resists, including liquid resists, are important for creating special effects, but are not used as commonly as sheet resists.

SHEET RESISTS

When working with sheet resists, you cover the entire surface of the glass, then cut and remove pieces of resist from the areas you wish to etch. Most resist materials have two layers: one is a sheet of resilient vinyl or rubber, coated with adhesive; the other is a wax- or silicone-coated paper or sheet plastic, which covers the adhesive side until you are ready to apply the resist.

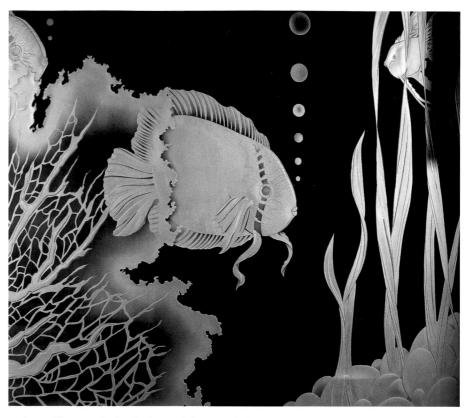

Barbara Lillian Boeck, detail of curved, laminated glass wall inset with edge lighting, overall size: 48" x 60" x ½". Carving and shading techniques.

The resist you choose for any particular job depends on the kind of etching you're doing and the type of glass you're using. See Chapters 5, 6 and 7 for information about resists appropriate for surface etching, carving and shading, respectively. For chemical etching, toughness is not an issue, since the resist takes little physical abuse during the etching process. However, it is important to use a resist that sticks to the glass well and doesn't let the etching cream get underneath. This does not require a costly resist, and inexpensive vinyls are the usual choice.

Hard Vinyl Resists

Hard vinyls are moderately tough and hold up beautifully for surface etching and shading. They can also be used—carefully—for carving. These resists are usually opaque white and come in 4-, 6- and 8-mil thicknesses and in rolls from 12" to 36" wide and 10 to 50 yards long.

The 4- and 6-mil hard vinyls are adequate for surface etching or shading. Hard vinyls 11 to 15 mils

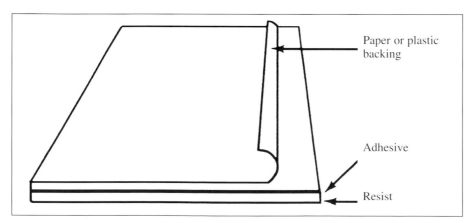

The silicone-coated paper or plastic backing protects the adhesive until the resist is applied to the glass.

Paper or plastic backing

Adhesive

Resist

thick are available, but are difficult to cut by hand; soft vinyl or rubber are better options when a thicker resist is required. The thinnest hard vinyls—the 4- and 6-mil—are perfectly adequate for chemical etching. Hard vinyls are the most reasonably priced resists.

Soft Vinyl Resists

Soft vinyl resists are available from 12 to 25 mils thick, and are very close in price and in cutting and blasting characteristics to the rubber resists. The only major difference is that soft vinyls are much more likely than rubber to shrink after a design is cut. This means that if you use a soft vinyl resist, you should complete the entire etching process within a few days of starting. If you don't, the resist may shrink away from the cut lines, causing distortions which can ruin your design.

Clear Vinyl

Clear vinyl resist is usually available in 4 or 8 mil thickness, and in rolls ranging from 18" to 24" wide and 10 to 50 yards long.

Because of its relative lack of toughness, clear vinyl resist is the least effective resist material on the market; the 8-mil is actually less resistant to blasting than a 6-mil white vinyl. Clear vinyl also does not respond well to any kind of design transfer process, and is particularly susceptible to failure when used for abrasive etching in temperatures of about 45°F or below (no winter etching in your garage!). For all these reasons, we seldom use or recommend it.

However, clear vinyl resist does have a few virtues. Because it's clear, you can place your drawing under the glass to which the resist is attached, and cut the design without tracing. Its transparency also makes it a good choice for re-masking areas which need addi-

Jean-Paul Raymond, *Le Poisson*, optical and blown glass, surface etched, deeply carved and gilded, 31½" x 15¾".

tional work after a first round of blasting.

Rubber Resists

These materials are the toughest on the market. This may seem counter-intuitive, since rubber is softer than vinyl—however, that's exactly why it's tougher. The soft surface is more resilient when bombarded by the abrasive stream; it can withstand higher pressures and longer blasting times than any other resist material.

Photo resists from several manufacturers, showing some of the stock designs available.

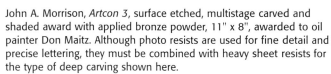

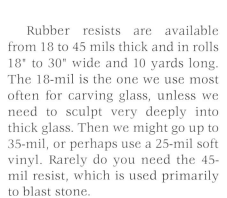

John A. Morrison, *Artcon 3*, surface etched, multistage carved and shaded award with applied bronze powder, 11" x 8", awarded to oil painter Don Maitz. Although photo resists are used for fine detail and precise lettering, they must be combined with heavy sheet resists for the type of deep carving shown here.

Rubber resists are available from 18 to 45 mils thick and in rolls 18" to 30" wide and 10 yards long. The 18-mil is the one we use most often for carving glass, unless we need to sculpt very deeply into thick glass. Then we might go up to 35-mil, or perhaps use a 25-mil soft vinyl. Rarely do you need the 45-mil resist, which is used primarily to blast stone.

Because of their softness, rubber resists are much easier to cut than hard vinyl. They are also the most expensive resist materials available. Rubber resists are particularly well suited for the graphite design transfers discussed later in the chapter.

Photo Resist

Photo resist is one of the latest advancements in resist technology. The design in a photo resist is not a photographic image, but rather a black-and-white image produced with a photographic process which allows very fine detail. The design is not only transferred to the resist, but also processed so that the elements to be blasted are removed. Because the resist is ready to apply and blast, this option can save considerable time by eliminating the need to enlarge, trace and hand cut a design.

The disadvantage of photo resists is their relatively high expense. They are most often used for small, highly complex patterns such as logos, text and designs on awards, trophies and gift items. Although all photo resists can be etched with abrasive blasting, most *cannot* be used with etching cream. A membrane that holds the design elements together while the resist is being applied prevents the cream from contacting the glass.

Photo resists can be custom made with your original design; stock designs can also be ordered from most manufacturers. Recent innovations include a new type of photo resist that you can produce in your own studio.

Precut Resists

Precut resists are another recent advancement. They are basically standard sheet resists (from 4- to 45-mil vinyl or rubber) with a design that is already drawn and cut. In that way, they are very similar to photo resists. The major difference is that with precut resists, no areas of the cut design have been removed. This allows you the choice of etching either the design or the background, depending on which part of the resist you remove. It also allows you to use precut designs with multistage carving or shading. With photo resists, you don't have these choices. Because the areas to be blasted are already removed, you can't choose which areas to etch.

Precut resists are less expensive than photo resists, and are great for designs with medium-fine detail. They're especially well suited for precise geometric and straight-line designs, and can reproduce finer detail than can be obtained with hand cutting, though not nearly as fine as with photo resists.

Like photo resists, precut resists can be custom made from your original design or ordered from a selection of designs offered by the manufacturer; see the list of suppliers in the Appendix. In contrast to photo resists, precut resists work very well with etching creams. While photo resists are always more expensive, the cost of precut resists varies widely, depending, in part, on the kind of resist material used and the size of the resist. Precut resists over two square feet can be less than half the cost of photo resists.

FOUND RESIST MATERIALS

Found resist materials are anything you find which will resist the etching process (if only for a short time), but which are not specifical-

A precut resist consists of a cover sheet, the resist itself (with precut design), and the backing sheet. Here, the cover sheet is peeled back and one precut element is lifted up.

ly made for etching. Look in your garage, on the ground at a construction site, in a hardware store—anywhere and everywhere. Consider using wire meshes and screens, old tennis rackets, leaves and plant parts, gloves, doilies and lace, plastic and silk flowers, wax, glue, latex paint and who knows what else! Let your imagination go.

Categories of Found Resists

- Materials inherently resistant to etching
- Liquids
- Materials that can be treated with liquids to make them resistant

Materials Inherently Resistant to Etching

This category includes such odd things as wire mesh, welded wire, fencing, gutter screen, expanded metal, plastic mesh, and plastic leaves and flowers. Unfortunately, these kinds of objects do not work well with chemical etching, since they don't adhere tightly to the glass surface and thus allow the etching cream to seep underneath. Items in this category can create some wonderful textures, but are obviously limited in application.

To attach these objects to the glass, tape their outside edges or

Found resist materials can be almost anything that will resist the etching process.

use temporary spray adhesive. If you're careful, you can hold the object with one hand and depend on the force of the blast to keep it in place. Be sure to hold the nozzle at a 90-degree angle over the glass surface, and don't blast over your fingers, or you'll find that they're outlined on the glass, too.

Liquid Resists

A liquid resist is applied as a liquid, but allowed to dry, and etched as a solid resist. The advantage of a liquid resist is that you can choose a method of application that produces a unique effect. You can paint the liquid on for a fluid, 'painterly' effect, or stipple it on with a brush, sponge or piece of

Welded wire mesh makes an effective resist.

crushed newspaper for an irregular texture or splotched effect. You might also dribble the resist onto the glass from a foot or two above and get a random splash pattern. These types of effects cannot be produced any other way.

At one time, liquid resists were the only types of resist materials used to etch glass, and they are still popular with artists who like to experiment. Asphaltum, shellac and wax can all be used as resists, with different effects. Asphaltum and shellac resist the etching process completely, yielding clean lines and boundaries. Their unwelcome aspects include strong odors and toxic clean-up materials, including mineral spirits and acetone. Wax

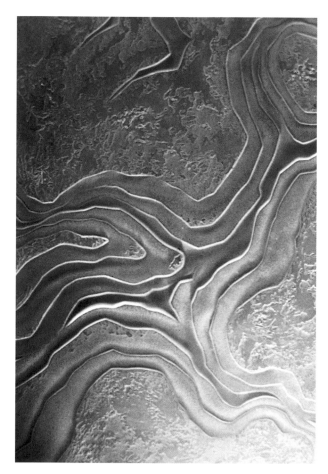
Degnan-Laurie Glassworks, detail of 40'L carved and textured glass wall in the corporate headquarters of Pitney, Harding, Kipp and Szuch, Morristown, NJ. Heavy resist was used for the undulating carved lines; a stippled liquid resist was used to produce the texture.

Ellen Abbott and Mark Leva, panel in stone base, surface etched, multistage carved and shaded, 5' x 5', collection of the artists. The circular "magnifying lenses" contain details produced by found resists—including lace and other fabrics—as well as white glue.

A test piece with found resist materials, etched with multistage shading.

resists produce soft, irregular edges as the wax wears away during the blasting process.

Latex paint and diluted white glue wear away during blasting, but full strength water soluable white glue can serve as a tough carving resist. A resist that breaks down during blasting is desirable in some cases; it leaves a slightly undulating, fuzzy edge that can't be obtained any other way. This can give a very realistic effect on subjects like tree trunks or coral. Both latex and glue are non-toxic and can be cleaned up easily with water. Like other water-soluble liquid resists, they cannot be used with etching cream, but are fine with abrasive blasting.

Another liquid resist that can be used effectively on round glassware is plastic tool dip. This is the stuff you buy at a hardware store and use to coat the handles of pliers when the original plastic coating comes off. Paint it on the glass surface in several layers; once

dried, it can be cut with a standard stencil knife. Plastic tool dip works fine with chemical etching. It's also fine for abrasive etching at light blasting pressures, but the high pressures used for carving will tear it off the glass.

Materials Which Can Be Made Resistant

Such unlikely things as paper doilies, cotton lace and other fabrics can be used as resists if saturated with a liquid like water-soluable white glue. These materials are placed on the glass surface while still wet, and allowed to harden before blasting. The paper or fabric provides the pattern, and the glue strengthens them so they can withstand the abrasive blast.

FALSE ECONOMY: RESISTS *NOT* TO USE

Many beginners try using inexpensive materials like contact paper, masking tape or duct tape as re-

sists. These are poor choices. They lift and wear down during abrasive etching, spoiling the lines of your pattern and creating a 'snow' effect where the abrasive penetrates the material. Furthermore, the adhesives in these materials are so aggressive that you're likely to break the glass as you try to remove the material. Finally, you have to contend with adhesive residue that remains on the glass after the 'resist' is removed. This residue must be removed with solvents such as mineral spirits and acetone, which are both expensive and hazardous to your health. Use them with all necessary precautions.

Applying the Resist

Before you attach the resist to the glass, take time (if you haven't already) to think about which glass surface you want to etch. This decision will effect the look and use of the glass, as well as the orientation of the design. Etching is usually done on the second surface of the glass—the side away from the viewer. Apply the resist to the side you plan to etch.

WHICH SIDE TO ETCH?

With flat glass, there is usually a choice of which surface to etch. Because the etched surface will be more difficult to clean, it should be mounted so that it's less likely to attract dirt, dust and fingerprints.

With three-dimensional glass, there usually isn't a choice. Because of small openings, it's difficult or impossible to etch the interiors of most glass vases. With glass tableware, etching the interior is impractical—especially if the piece will be used to hold liquids—because of the difficulty of cleaning the etched surface. When it *is* possible to etch the inside, as with a

Eric Hilton, *Double Threshold*, multistage carved plate glass door in steel frame, private residence, Dallas, TX, 96" x 48" x 3". The artist has carved the entire surface of this door, using a tough resist to withstand extended exposure to the abrasive stream.

APPLYING SHEET RESIST TO FLAT GLASS

Begin by cutting a piece of resist about 1/2" longer and wider than the glass. Don't try to cut to the exact size of your glass; you'll never manage to get it on just right, and will have to patch where it's misaligned.

Peel about 1" of the backing paper off one edge of the resist and crease it so it won't close back up over the adhesive. Starting from the right side (if you are right-handed), hold the edge of the resist with the exposed adhesive just above the glass surface and position the resist on the glass. Make sure it covers the glass completely, then adhere the resist to the glass all along the right edge. Once this is in place, the resist cannot become misaligned.

Use a squeegee to affix the resist firmly to the glass and to prevent air bubbles.

glass bowl, the usual choice is still to etch the outside, since the interior will attract dust and dirt more quickly.

Etching tends to look better on the second surface because of the way it picks up light. The view of the etching through the glass is enhanced by reflections from the first surface, which highlight the thick-ness of the glass and show the depth of cut at the edge of the design. This is particularly true with carving, because of the greater depth of cut. Remember that any time the etching is done on the second surface, the pattern should be reversed so that it will read correctly when viewed from the front.

With your left hand, peel more of the backing paper. With your right hand, use a squeegee to smooth the resist onto the glass as you pull the paper away. This may take some practice. You need to exert a good amount of pressure with the squeegee to avoid trapping air bubbles. Because of the downward pressure, it's important that the

Tohru Okamura, *Tenku No Tsubasa*, multistage-carved blown glass bowl, 15"Dia x 7"H. Detailed multistage carving on a compound curved surface.

surface you are working on be very clean; any debris may cause the glass to scratch or even to break.

Air Bubbles

Once all of the backing paper is removed and the resist is completely attached to the glass, use a stencil knife to trim the resist flush with the edges of the glass. Look to see if air bubbles have been trapped anywhere under the resist. You'll want to avoid this; abrasives can puncture the resist over a bubble much more quickly than where the resist adheres completely.

Try to squeeze out any air bubbles with the squeegee. If that doesn't work, try peeling the resist back to where the bubbles appear, and then use the squeegee to reattach it to the glass. If the bubbles are trapped more than 5" or 6" in from the edge of the resist, you may have to puncture the air bubbles with your stencil knife, squeeze the air out, and then tape over any puncture marks with masking tape. This can take a long time if you have many bubbles, and there is always the risk of the tape coming off, allowing the abrasive or etching cream to etch the area.

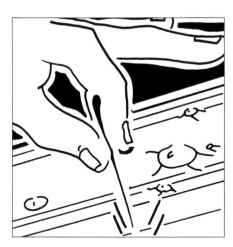

Puncture air bubbles larger than $1/8$" with a needle or stencil knife, then patch any visible holes with masking tape or resist.

Sometimes it's sensible to postpone dealing with air bubbles until the design is transferred and cut. If you cut across or close to an air bubble when you cut the design, you can squeeze the air out easily. However, too many bubbles will make it hard to transfer your design accurately. With practice, it is easy to apply resist with no bubbles; the time you take learning to do this will be well spent.

APPLYING SHEET RESIST TO CURVED GLASS

You'll encounter two basic shapes as you work with curved glass. The first is curved only around the side, or circumference, of the form—as with a cylinder or cone shape. This glassware can be thought of as having a 'simple' curve.

The second is curved along the profile of the form, as well as the circumference—as with a wine goblet or brandy snifter. Other than flat-sided pieces like square vases, all glassware has the first type of curve. Glassware that is curved both around the circumference and along the profile is said to have a 'compound' curve.

Working with Simple Curves

Glass objects with simple curves present no real problem when applying resist. Use a resist appropriate for the kind of etching you'll be doing, measure the height and circumference of the glass, and cut a piece of resist that's slightly larger.

Peel about 1" of backing paper from the 'tall' side of the resist—the side that will be applied to the height of the glass—and attach the resist. If the glass is too large to hold comfortably in your hand, lay it down on a soft towel folded several times to make a thick 'bed.' This will prevent the glass from rolling as you apply the resist.

As you pull the backing paper out from under the resist, you'll create a tension that will cause the resist to adhere firmly to the glass, with few or no air bubbles. Use your squeegee only if you have problems with bubbles. The resist should cover the entire surface, overlapping slightly at the edge where you started. Excess resist at the top and bottom of the glass can be folded over onto the glass, or trimmed off.

If your object has a handle, apply the resist there separately.

Working with Compound Curves

With pieces that have a compound curve, use only soft vinyl or rubber resist, since these resists stretch

APPLYING RUBBER RESIST TO A VASE WITH COMPOUND CURVES

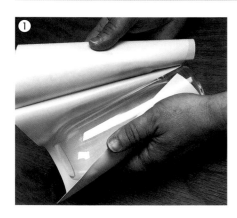

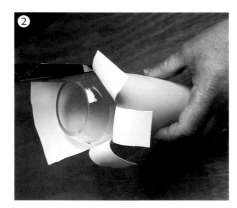

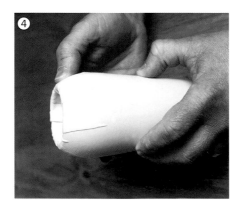

1 Cut a piece of resist somewhat larger than the area you need to cover.
2 Cut slits where the resist needs to conform to the compound curve.
3 Fold the individual pieces of resist down over each other one at a time.
4 Check for air bubbles or areas not covered by resist.

easily. Cut a piece of resist 1/4" to 1/2" larger than the design. Peel off the backing paper and, working on a folded towel, apply the resist to the area of the glass where you want the design etched. Holding the resist at either end, allow the center to sag down and touch the glass. Then, working progressively from the center outward, allow the resist to touch more and more of the glass surface.

When about half of the resist is touching the glass, release it gently. Starting from the middle and working outward to the edges, press the resist firmly down onto the glass with your thumbs. Squeeze air bubbles out as you go.

Gently stretch the resist to cover the convex area of the glass. Where the glass is concave, there will be puckers in the edge of the resist. Cut a slit into each pucker with your stencil knife; fold down the flaps, one on top of the other.

Once the resist in the design area is firmly attached, cut strips of resist to cover areas of the glass which are still exposed. Apply the

Laurie Thal and Melissa Malm, *Aurora Sunflowers*, etched blown glass vase with flashed surface color, 11"Dia x 8"H. The color change on this bowl comes from etching away a flashed layer of color on the surface to reveal the clear glass underneath.

strips, overlapping slightly. Once the glass is covered completely, transfer the design as best you can with one of the techniques mentioned below. This will be some-what difficult with compound curves, since the overlapping pieces of resist create an uneven surface. Unfortunately, there's just no easy way to do this.

Ruth Dobbins, *Vitroglyphs*™, ©1994, glassware. Prototypes for design additions to an existing product line, using hand-cut rubber resist. Ruth designs directly on the glass after the resist is applied.

Applying a Precut or Photo Resist With a Tape Hinge

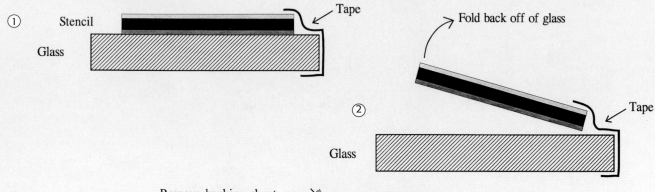

① Stencil — Tape

Glass

Fold back off of glass

② — Tape

Glass

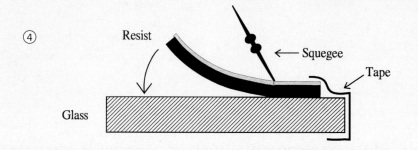

③ Remove backing sheet →

Adhesive side of resist

Glass ← Tape

④ Resist

Squegee → Tape

Glass

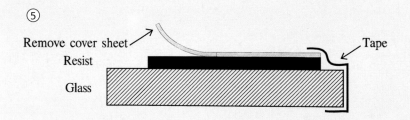

⑤ Remove cover sheet → Tape

Resist

Glass

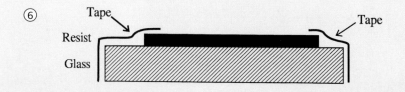

⑥ Tape Tape

Resist

Glass

1 Position the resist on the glass and tape it in place along the length of one edge.

2 Fold the resist back, using the tape as a hinge.

3 Remove the backing sheet to expose the adhesive on the back of the resist.

4 Apply the resist to the glass with a squeegee. Start from the tape and work toward the opposite edge.

5 Remove the cover sheet; the attached tape will come off, too.

6 Tape the edges of the resist to cover any exposed glass. You're then ready to blast (if using a photo resist) or selectively remove resist elements (if using a precut resist).

Laurie Thal and Melissa Malm, *Cobalt–Ruby Lotus* (detail).

Laurie Thal and Melissa Malm, *Cobalt–Ruby Lotus*, blown glass vase with flashed surface color, 13"Dia x 7"H. The multistage shading technique controls the color change in the lotus petals so that they can touch each other without losing definition.

APPLYING PRECUT AND PHOTO RESISTS

Precut resists and photo resists have to be applied somewhat differently than regular sheet resists. This is because the design is already cut.

Both photo resists and precut resists are made in three layers instead of two, as with other sheet resists. The resist material itself is the middle layer, with a cover sheet on one side and a backing sheet on the other. The backing sheet covers and protects the adhesive side of the resist until you are ready to apply it. The cover sheet holds the stencil together (since it is already cut) as you peel off the backing paper to expose the adhesive, and as you apply the resist to the glass.

There are several methods of applying these resists. The first is used when precise alignment or positioning is not required and when the resist is relatively small (about 8" x 10" or smaller). Pull the backing paper off, position the stencil over the glass, and lay it down carefully on the clean glass. Squeegee it firmly in place, then remove the cover sheet. Tape around the outside edges with sheet resist or a good-quality masking tape to cover the remaining areas of exposed glass.

The Tape-Hinge Method

When exact alignment and positioning are required, we suggest the tape-hinge method of attaching resist. With this technique, you use a ruler to position the resist pre-

Precut resists and photo resists have three layers (side view).

cisely where you want the image etched. While holding the resist in position, apply a strip of masking tape to one edge of the resist. Fold the resist all the way back, using the tape as a hinge. Remove the backing paper and reapply the resist to the glass, using the squeegee to press it in place. Work from the tape hinge toward the opposite edge of the glass.

The Wet Application Method

The wet application technique works only with precut resists. Mix one or two drops of clear liquid dishwashing soap into a quart of water in a spray bottle. Spray the surface of the glass with a light, fine mist of the soap-and-water solution. Remove the backing paper and lay the resist down on the glass. Slide the resist into position on the wet glass (use a ruler to check placement, if necessary). Hold the resist with one hand and squeegee it with the other, squeezing the water from under the resist as you go. This will allow the adhesive to begin to hold.

Leave the project for at least 24 hours, so all the water evaporates. Then go over the resist once more with a squeegee to make sure the adhesive is firmly attached to the glass.

The wet application method works with precut resist because neither the resist nor the adhesive is water soluble. It doesn't work with photo resist, which will soften with exposure to water, and gradually disintegrate.

All of these methods will work on flat or curved glass. The only problem you might encounter is applying precut or photo resist to a surface with a compound curve. In that case, since it is not possible to cut the resist into strips, the size of the design must be kept fairly small.

WORKING WITH A PRECUT STENCIL

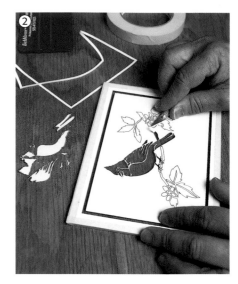

1 A tape hinge is useful for applying precut resist to flat glass.
2 Just peel the precut elements, and you're ready to blast or use etching cream.

WORKING WITH A PHOTO RESIST

1 Apply the resist to a bottle by bending it down in the middle until it touches. Press it along the curve with a squeegee or your fingers.
2 Remove the clear cover sheet, then tape the rest of the exposed glass around the resist before blasting.

Jean Paul Raymond, *Colonne Solaire*, polished, cut and multistage-carved optical glass, 10" x 10" x 31½".

4

Design

Designs used for surface etching, carving and shading
have different—and impor-
tant—specific requirements. Understanding those requirements is key to
your success with any of the techniques. In this chapter we'll cover
the kind of design needed for each
technique, as well as the fine points
of resizing designs and converting
them from block to line drawings—
and vice versa. Finally, we'll look at
several techniques for transferring
designs to resist and cutting the
transferred design. These are the
last steps before etching.

Design Function

A good glass etching always starts
with a design, usually drawn on paper. The design (or 'pattern') serves
two major purposes. First, it's a
full-size picture of the finished
piece. It allows you to think on paper, working out details of the project before you cut into the resist or
alter the glass surface. With multistage carving and multistage shading, the design is also a tool for
planning the sequence of elements
to peel and blast.

The second function of a design
is to give you exact lines to follow
when cutting the resist with your
stencil knife. This means that the

Margaret Oldman, *Sea Dreams*, multistage shaded and surface etched panel with neon illumination, 28" x 23".

final pattern should be a finished drawing, not a rough sketch.

With surface etching and carving, one pattern can perform both functions (see Chapters 5 and 6). With shading, however, it's often best to have a separate pattern for each function. Here's why. In order to determine the correct sequence of elements to peel and blast, a shading pattern must first be rendered, or shaded. Sometimes the exact lines between elements get blurred in the process, making the pattern difficult to use as a template for cutting.

Styles of Design

Two basic types of patterns are used with abrasive glass etching: block designs and line drawings. Block designs are used for single-stage etching, like surface etching or single-stage carving. Line designs are used for multistage carving and multistage shading.

BLOCK DESIGNS

The kind of design that best utilizes the visual qualities of surface etching is a block design, as opposed to a line drawing. This is because surface etching creates just two visual elements: the dark effect of clear glass and the light effect of the etched surface. In a block design, each individual element is a solid color, and all elements are separated by a space. In contrast, elements in a line drawing touch, and cannot be filled with color because the distinctions between elements would be lost.

Stencil Patterns

Although few books feature designs specifically for glass etching, books of block designs are available at art supply stores, book stores and libraries. Many of these are in

A block design is the pattern style needed for surface etching. All elements are filled with solid color, and each is separate from the others.

The same design converted to a line drawing, the pattern style needed for multistage carving and shading. A line drawing shows all elements touching.

A stencil design is a block design with wide spaces between elements (and between the elements and the background).

Stencil designs can be improved for glass etching by retracing to make spaces between elements smaller. Fill elements with color so you can easily see which should be peeled.

stencil format. Although stencil designs are block designs, stencils always have 'bridges' between the floating elements to hold the stencil together after it's cut out. Also, the spaces between elements are relatively large to increase the strength of the cut stencil. Neither bridges nor large spaces are necessary for surface etching; in fact, they make the designs look unnecessarily clumsy.

Stencil designs can be used for surface etching, but we recommend that you retrace the design to narrow the spaces between elements and eliminate the bridges. This will give your finished piece a more delicate and realistic look.

Although all stencil designs are block designs, not all block designs are stencil designs. You should be able to find good block designs that can be etched without modification; see the Appendix for sources. And, of course, you can make your own block designs.

LINE DRAWINGS

Line drawings for glass etching are sometimes called 'outline drawings,' because they outline each element, defining the edges and common lines between elements. Line drawings are used for both multistage carving and multistage shading since design elements *do* touch with these techniques. Like block designs, line drawings serve as cutting patterns as the designs are cut in the resist.

When elements of a line drawing are peeled off the glass, no bits of resist remain to separate them. Instead, the cut line at the edge of an element also serves as the edge of the next element. With nothing separating elements from each other, the distinction between them must be created at the time of etching. This is done by peeling and blasting in stages. (If all elements were peeled and etched at the same time, the result would be a silhouette, with no distinction between elements at all).

Converting Designs

You may find a line drawing that you'd like to convert to a block design, or vice versa. This isn't particularly difficult, but it does take some practice.

LINE DRAWING TO BLOCK DESIGN

Converting a line drawing to a block design serves two functions. First, it makes it possible to etch the image without losing detail. In addition, it forces you to visualize which areas should be blasted and which remain clear. This enables

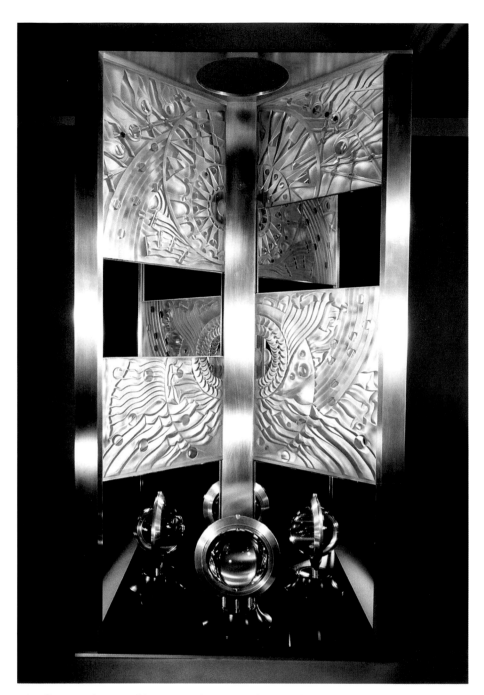

Eric Hilton, *Northstar*, multistage carved mirrors in lacquered metal frame, 48" x 31" x 14", for the Royal Caribbean Cruise Line. Carved, angled mirrors give an illusion of expanded size and depth.

you to work quickly and confidently as you cut and remove the resist.

There are a couple of simple ways to convert a line design to a block design.

Tracing Paper—Tape your design to a light table (or a window, during the day), and cover it with tracing paper. Trace around the inside of each element, leaving a little space between elements. The amount of space depends on how large the design is, and the distance from which it will be viewed

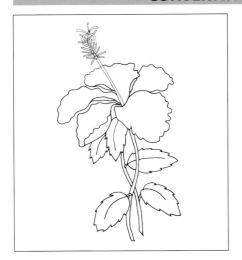

The original line drawing.

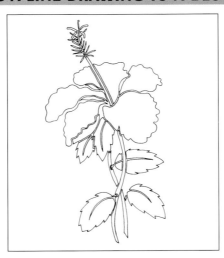

Retrace each element on the inside of each line, leaving space between elements.

Fill in the elements so that it's easier to remove the correct elements for etching. This also enables you to see what the design will look like when finished.

most often. Generally, spaces between elements should range from $1/16"$ to $1/4"$.

Carbon Paper—Place your original design on a piece of carbon paper which is face-down on a sheet of blank paper. Draw over the outlines of each element on the original design, leaving spaces between elements as mentioned above.

Whichever process you use, it's a good idea to fill in the elements you want to blast with solid color. If you don't, you'll simply have a line drawing with double lines between elements. It may be difficult to actually 'see' the design and know which areas are to be peeled and blasted, and which are not.

BLOCK DESIGN TO LINE DRAWING

If you want to carve or shade a block design, you must first convert it to a line drawing.

Both carving and shading depend on elements touching each other; distinctions between elements are created by the contrast of how much each element is blast-

ed compared to other elements at the point where they touch. Because elements don't touch at all in a block design, this type of drawing is useless for multistage work.

To convert a block design into a line drawing, you can use either tracing paper or carbon paper as described above, but with one major difference. To create a line design, you'll need to trace a line around each element that is slightly *larger* than the element and parallel to the edges of the element. In fact, the line should extend half the distance between any elements that would normally touch. Make sure there's just one line—not two—between elements that touch. It may help to think of a block design as an expanded or 'exploded' line drawing; a line drawing is a block design that has been put back together.

Sizing Designs

No matter what etching technique you use, or what style of design, you will invariably need to change

the size of your pattern. In most cases, you'll start with small designs and need to enlarge them, but occasionally you will also need to reduce a design that is too large.

There are several ways to customize the size of your design. The method you choose will be dictated by the equipment available to you, the style of the design, and its ultimate destination. If you are working with a design where precise straight lines and symmetry are important, you can save time by having the size adjustment done by a blueprint company, and enjoy the security of knowing that you're working with a near-perfect resizing.

Resizing Technology

- Photocopier
- Blueprint
- Projection
- Opaque
- Overhead
- Slide
- Computer and scanner
- Pantograph
- Grid system

Left: Tohru Okamura, *Aroma*, crystal vase, surface etched. This delicate block design makes good use of the black-and-white graphic effect of surface etching.

Below: Duncan Laurie, *Jokasta*, carved plate glass sculpture, wood base, 24" x 18". Single-stage carved elements, like the borders of this piece, are best represented on the pattern by block elements, while the multistage shaded elements in the center are drawn as line designs.

PHOTOCOPIER

By far the most commonly used resizing technology is the copy machine. Most copiers have enlargement and reduction capabilities, though many are limited to an 11" x 17" output. For larger projects, you'll have to tape several pieces of paper together for the final pattern.

Copy machine enlargements will sometimes distort your design. This can be frustrating if you are piecing together several sheets of paper, because lines from one sheet may not line up exactly with the continued lines on the next. With organic designs and designs with irregular line quality, this may not be critical, but with precise or geometric designs, your patience may be tested. Happily, the larger copy centers now have copiers that can handle paper up to 2' x 3'. This eliminates paste-ups on many projects and makes paste-ups on larger projects much easier.

Another drawback with this technology is that designs which are greatly enlarged will have very wide lines. You'll have to approximate as you transfer your pattern and cut your resist.

BLUEPRINT

If you want very large patterns to be all in one piece, you'll have to go to a blueprint shop. This option can be somewhat expensive, particularly if the enlargement must be done in several steps, requiring a number of copies. On the other hand, it will save you a lot of time. Blueprint shops can enlarge your design to almost any size.

Like copier enlargements, blueprints which are much larger than the original drawing will have very wide lines. Fresh blueprints have a distinct ammonia smell. It's unpleasant and takes a few days to dissipate.

Barbara Lillian Boeck, solarium doors, surface etched and multistage carved laminated safety glass, 30" x 72" x ½". Both block and line design styles were used in the pattern for these doors.

PROJECTORS

Opaque, overhead and slide projectors can all be used to both reduce and enlarge designs, but reducing a design is most easily done with a slide projector. When using any kind of projector, start with a piece of paper that has the perimeter of your resized design drawn on it. Tape or pin the paper to the wall, and move the projector closer to or further from the paper until the projected image fits into the design perimeter.

To avoid distorting your design, arrange the projector 'square' to the paper so the image is projected horizontally, rather than at an angle. In other words, the distance from the floor to the projection lens should be the same as the distance from the floor to the center of the projected design. If you project up an angle, the top of the image will be wider than the bottom. You may need to raise the projector by putting boxes beneath it.

Heather Robyn Matthews, *Heron & Alligator*, free-standing multistage carved and shaded plate glass panel, 48" x 60" x ¾", photo: Tim Matthews. In a complex design like this, elements are distinguished from each other by the depth (multistage carving) or density (multistage shading) of blast they receive.

It's important to trace over a smooth surface. If the wall is rough, position a piece of masonite, smooth plywood, or wallboard against it to create a smooth surface.

If you don't own a projector, you may be able to rent or borrow one from a stained glass supply shop, library, school or office supply store. You may also find one at a rental

company that carries audio visual equipment. Policies vary; you'll need to find out whether you can take the projector home with you on a rental basis, or must use it at the facility that owns it.

All of the projection techniques require time and effort on your part, but they can save money if the equipment is readily available. Renting any kind of projector will

Norm and Ruth Dobbins, reverse surface etched bathroom windows, each panel 12" x 18". Decorative reverse etching can be used to block a view.

cost about as much as enlarging your design at a copy center or blueprint shop. Of course, you can always save up designs and enlarge several at the same time.

Opaque Projector

With most opaque projectors, your original drawing cannot be larger than 8" x 10". Project your design onto the piece of paper and—standing at an angle so you don't block the projected image—trace your enlarged design.

Using an opaque projector is time consuming and awkward, but it will give you what you need. If you find that you use this kind of projector often, it may be a worthwhile purchase. Opaque projectors can be found at art supply stores. Prices vary widely, as does quality.

Overhead Projector

Overhead projectors are used by business firms and schools for presentations. You should be able to borrow one from these sources or rent one from a rental company.

When using an overhead projector, your original drawing must be on clear acetate. This means you must either draw directly on acetate with specially-designed pens, or have your design transferred to a special acetate available at copy centers. Your acetate original can be no larger than $8^1/_2$" x 11".

The primary problem with opaque and overhead projectors is that their projected images aren't very bright. You must have access to a room where you can leave the lights off until you finish tracing.

Slide Projector

If you have a good slide of your design, you can use a slide projector for resizing. This is an excellent resizing method, since slide projectors project a much brighter image than opaque or overhead projectors, and can be used in a room

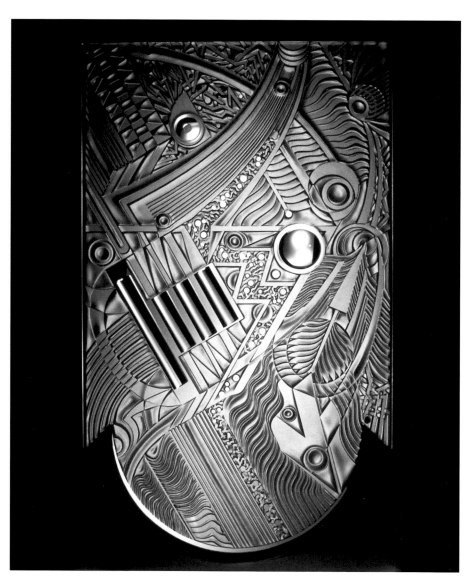

Eric Hilton, *Tidal Pull*, multistage-carved plate glass with cut and polished optical crystal elements and aluminum frame, 36" x 23" x 10", collection of Vitro, Monterey, Mexico.

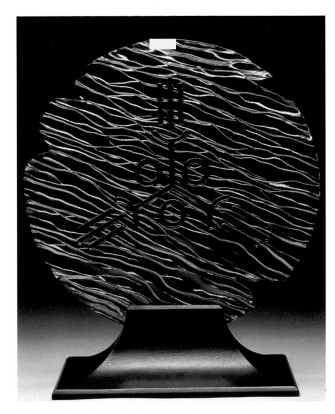

John Morrison, *Future Antique*, plate glass sculpture, carved on both sides, 18"D x 28"H. The carved areas have been clear coated to remove the frosted look.

Bonnie Brown, *Maggie Magnolia*, multistage carved and shaded design with gold leafing on limestone base, 18" x 30", photo: Mel Schockner.

with the windows uncovered or with lights on.

Another advantage of using a slide projector is that your original design can be larger than 8½" x 11", since you can take a slide of a much larger piece of paper. A disadvantage is that the slide film is only about 7/8" x 1 3/8". When that tiny image is projected up to door-panel size, it's enlarged about 4,000 percent. This maximizes the possibility of distortion, especially with geometric designs that have sharp angles and straight lines.

COMPUTER AND SCANNER

The most sophisticated way to deal with size adjustments is by using a computer and scanner. Once scanned, your design should be imported into an image-manipulation program such as CorelDRAW or Adobe Illustrator.

A scanned image can be problematical. As you enlarge it, the line width will enlarge as well, and the lines will become increasingly jagged. To avoid these problems, you can convert your design to a *vector* image, which can take considerable time. You'll probably have to retrace or redraw the complete image in the computer, and then 'clean up' the electronic image to make it accurate. The amount of time required depends on the complexity of the design and the extent to which the image must be enlarged; it can amount to several hours. We recommend this step only if you intend to use the design several times.

Printing a Scanned Design

After the image is cleaned up, you can enlarge or reduce it to any size with no increase in line width. The only limitation then becomes the size of the paper your printer can

Wendy Saxon-Brown, *Jugglers*, multistage carved plate glass with applied surface color in some etched elements, 26" x 17". The contour of the top edge was achieved through carving.

handle. For large images you'll have to piece together several sheets of paper. This isn't difficult to do, since there's no distortion in the printouts as there is with copy-machine enlargements.

If you have access to a plotter (a device used for outputting architectural plans in line format), the entire image can often be output directly. The size limitation here is the width of the plotter, usually a generous 18" to 36". Most software allows you to output designs of any length when using a plotter.

Advantages:
- Easy adjustment of size and design
- Neat and professional presentation form
- No need to store large drawings

Disadvantages:
- Cost of the equipment and software
- Long learning curve for software
- Time-consuming process

PANTOGRAPH

The old-fashioned way to enlarge a pattern is with a pantograph. These inexpensive devices are still available in many art supply stores. They provide a mechanical proportioning arm that enlarges the design on a separate piece of paper as you trace over the original by hand. Learning to use a pantograph is tricky, but they get the job done.

GRID SYSTEM

A grid system is the ultimate in low-tech, hand-enlargement techniques. You draw a full-size box for your enlargement and divide both your original and your enlarged box into the same number of squares. You then enlarge the elements in each square, one at a time, from your original into the corresponding square on your enlargement.

With grid enlargements, you need no equipment beyond a pencil and ruler, but the process is time consuming and the results are never precise. Use this method selectively.

Transferring Your Design to Resist

Once you have selected and prepared your design, you'll need to transfer it to resist and cut it out.

Architectural Glass Design, Gordon Huether, detail of a surface etched and shaded window with appliquéd dichroic glass, photo: Michael Brok. The artist scanned pine needles to create the background pattern.

There are several transfer techniques. Some work better with one type of resist than another, and all can be used with varying success on curved glass, as well as flat.

- Clear resist
- Carbon paper
- Graphite transfer
- Spray adhesive
- Photocopy transfer on repro film
- Photo resist and precut resist

CLEAR RESIST

With clear vinyl resist, you can simply slide your drawing under the glass piece and cut the lines while viewing them through the resist. Some people like this method, but the results can be somewhat inaccurate because of a phenomenon known as *parallax*. Parallax (from the Greek word for 'change') accounts for the apparent displacement of a line seen through glass when viewed from an angle. It's more of a problem glass that's 1/4" thick or thicker.

To avoid having lines out of place when cutting with clear resist, you must look straight down on the design while you cut. This can become tedious. On curved glass, simply place the design inside the glass and cut with the resist on the outside.

CARBON PAPER

If you are using a white vinyl resist, carbon paper provides a good, basic—though time-consuming—transfer method. Position your drawing on the resist where you want the design to be on the glass. Tape it down in two spots along one edge and then slide a sheet of carbon paper, face down, between the design and the resist. Tape the drawing down on the opposite edge and start tracing.

When you think the tracing is complete, lift the tape at one point only and look carefully beneath the carbon paper. If you missed any portion of the design, you can lay it back down and finish tracing. Don't remove all the tape at once; it will be nearly impossible to reposition the drawing accurately.

Now you can remove the carbon paper and the drawing from the resist. Depending on the grade of carbon paper used, you may find it necessary to spray the transferred design with a fixative, so it won't smudge while cutting. This sealer is available from art supply stores.

GRAPHITE TRANSFER

If your original drawing was made with a soft pencil, the best way to transfer it to rubber resist is with

Skyline Design, Mark Stegen, floral glass sculpture, multistage carved and shaded design on several layers of glass, with applied color, 72" x 30", photo: Marc Stegen. Layers of individually etched glass give a unique effect of depth.

the graphite transfer method. This works best with a drawing pencil, such as a 2B or 4B (available from art supply stores).

Place your drawing face down on the resist and tape it to the glass in a couple of places. Rub the back of the design with your squeegee or any hard object. This will transfer the pencil lines to the resist quickly and accurately. After removing the pattern, you're ready to cut. An advantage of this method is that you can usually count on three or four transfers with each design. This really saves time if you are making several projects with the same design.

With vinyl resists, you'll have varying success using graphite transfer, depending upon the specific vinyl and the softness of your pencil. Hard vinyls don't take a graphite transfer well; soft vinyls do. It's best to test a scrap before starting a real project. It's also important to keep in mind that this method will reverse your image. This is desirable for carving projects, since you'll almost always prefer to carve from one side and view from the other. For other

Wendy Saxon-Brown, *Chess*, multistage carved plate glass with applied surface color in some etched elements, 27" x 15".

kinds of techniques, it may or may not be desirable. Plan accordingly.

Spray Adhesive

This technique, which offers another way to avoid tracing, works well only if you have a simple design and a sharp blade in your stencil knife! Just spray the back of your drawing with temporary spray adhesive (available from art supply stores) and press it to the resist. Now you can take your stencil knife and cut through both the drawing and the resist.

Once you've finished cutting, remove the remaining paper from the resist. (That's the reason for using a temporary adhesive.) If paper is left on the resist as you blast, it will shred and mix with the abrasive. This will cause a problem when the abrasive is reused, since the paper absorbs moisture and can clog the blaster.

When using spray adhesive, be sure to make a copy of your design before cutting. Otherwise, it will be lost forever!

Photocopy Transfer on Repro Film

An alternative to the spray adhesive method is to copy your design onto architectural repro film. This thin, clear material has an adhesive already on it, and will easily adhere to your resist while you cut. Once the design is cut, you simply blast over the film that remains on the resist. The main disadvantage of this technique—for large projects—is its fairly high cost.

Photo Resist and Precut Resist

Photo resists and precut resists are great time savers. Since the design is already on the resist, no transfer is necessary.

Bonnie Brown, *Kimono Rack*, movable room divider, multistage carved and shaded plate glass on faux finished metal stand, 60" x 73½" x 23", photo: Jay Graham.

Cutting the Design

Beginning glass etchers often believe that the actual etching of the glass, whether abrasive or chemical, is the most important part of the process. The steps of enlarging, transferring and cutting the design may seem like no more than a necessary nuisance.

Nothing could be further from the truth. In any type of etching, the quality of the finished piece is in direct relationship to the care taken and the choices made at every step along the way. This is particularly true of the cutting process. Any mistakes in cutting are readily visible in the finished piece. Parallel lines that aren't parallel, straight lines that aren't straight, incorrect shapes of familiar objects—none of these may seem like a big deal when you're cutting, but they really stand out in the finished piece. So take time to double check your cut-and-peeled design before beginning to blast. What you see here is what you'll get in the final etching.

CUTTING TOOLS

The tool you'll use to cut out your design is a common stencil knife. These are available in a choice of several different handle sizes and blade shapes. They are inexpensive, so you may want to try several styles to see which you prefer. We suggest a knife about the size of a pencil. A round handle is important because you'll want to rotate it in your fingers for faster, more accurate cutting.

The blade you use with your stencil knife should be straight and come to a sharp point. We prefer a standard #11 blade; it's easy to use and inexpensive. Some experienced etchers swear by swivel knives, which have blades that rotate in the shaft of the knife as you cut. Others find these difficult to keep aligned on the pattern, since the knife point is offset from the shaft. Swivel knives are somewhat expensive, and only the best ones, with small blades and ball bearing swivels, are worth considering.

Electric hot-stencil cutters are also available, but they leave a fairly wide cut line and little nubs of melted resist if you pull them through the resist too fast. They are best on thin vinyls; don't try them with thick vinyls or on rubber materials.

With any kind of knife, it's important to use a sharp blade at all times, so keep spare ones on hand. A dull blade slows you down and does not produce a sharp, clean cut. You may be surprised at how fast you go through blades, especially when you're just starting out. If you'll be doing a lot of cutting, consider blades in packs of one hundred.

CUTTING TECHNIQUE

To cut the pattern, simply put the knife point down on one of the

Joan Irving, carved, surface-etched perfume bottle with applied color, made from ¾" plate glass, 12" x 4" x 2", photo: Ken West. The sandblaster has been used to carve this piece into the desired shape; it also textured the glass surface to hold the applied color.

Tools for cutting sheet resist materials. From the top: three swivel knives, three standard stencil knives, a set of five parallel line cutters with different line widths, a scalpel. Scalpels are not recommended for cutting resist; the flat handle is impossible to rotate in your fingers, and the curved blade does not give accurate cuts.

HOLDING YOUR STENCIL KNIFE

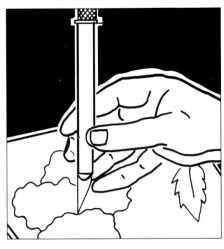

If you hold your stencil knife like a pencil, your cutting will be less accurate and slower. You'll also have to move the glass around frequently while cutting.

Try holding the stencil knife straight up and down, so you can swivel the knife in your fingers as you cut. This takes some practice, but it's a far better approach.

lines to be cut, and trace the line all around the element with the knife. Cut through the resist and down to the glass surface as you go. For straight lines, use a metal straight edge; it's almost impossible to cut perfectly straight lines free-hand.

As you cut, it may seem necessary to pick up the knife to change directions, or move the glass around on the table for a better angle. This is probably because you are holding the knife like a pencil. A much better way—one that will allow you to cut more quickly and more accurately—is to hold the knife perpendicular to the glass, between your thumb and first two or three fingers. With the knife in this position, you can swivel it to change directions without having to pick the point up off the glass. This helps ensure that the line is cut all the way around each element, rather than leaving little uncut bridges in the corners. It takes a good deal of practice to master this technique, but it will double your cutting speed once you do.

Last but not least, after all the cutting and peeling are complete, it's advisable to go back over the resist on the glass with a squeegee to make sure all corners and edges are firmly affixed to the glass. This will re-attach any resist that has been loosened by the peeling of adjacent pieces. Since too much pressure with the squeegee can itself scrape the remaining resist loose, it's wise to cover the resist with the backing paper or other paper before using the squeegee.

Surface Etching

Surface etching is the simplest form of glass etching—easy to learn and easy to do. In describing it as simple, however, we don't mean to suggest that surface etching is not worth learning or that you won't find many uses for it, even after you've learned the other techniques. Surface etching is simple only in contrast to the more involved processes of multistage carving and shading. Because you can achieve beautiful and intricate effects with surface etching, and because it's quick to learn and provides quick results, this is the technique almost everyone starts with.

Two Approaches

Surface etching can be accomplished in these two ways:

Abrasive Blasting—Also called 'abrasive etching,' 'sandblasting' or simply 'blasting,' this process requires a sandblaster, air compressor and blasting cabinet. It creates a bright, white surface that contrasts beautifully with the unetched glass.

Etching Cream—Chemical etching cream provides a great introduction to surface etching and requires almost no equipment. It produces a duller finish than blasting and appears gray-white in contrast to the unetched surface.

Ruth and Norm Dobbins, surface-etched ¼" glass panel in wood stand, part of a commercial product line, 9" x 12".

A third approach to surface etching involves the use of hydrofluoric acid. Because this substance is extremely dangerous, we cannot recommend its use. However, we have shown acid-etched projects in this chapter.

This chapter covers:
- principles of surface etching;
- appropriate designs, resists and glass;
- the step-by-step surface-etching process.

The sample projects included with this chapter allow you to walk through various processes while having us—in a sense—at your elbow. Patterns for these and other projects throughout the book are included in the Appendix. We urge you to try the projects; they'll give you a good feel for each of the techniques presented before you use them with your own designs.

Ruth and Norm Dobbins, *Indian Blanket*, surface-etched windows in private residence. The design in the lower half, etched as a positive, is mirrored in the top half in reverse etch. This is an effective approach for blocking an unwanted view outside the window while letting light into the room.

Overview of Surface-Etching Process

- Cover the glass completely with resist.
- Transfer the design to the resist.
- Cut out the design with a stencil knife.
- Peel areas of the design to be etched, exposing the clear glass beneath.
- Blast exposed glass in a blasting cabinet, or apply etching cream according to the manufacturer's directions.
- Carefully peel the remaining resist and clean the glass.

Principles of Surface Etching

Three basic principles define surface etching. First, as the name implies, the etching only affects the surface of the glass and has a density of 100 percent. If the etching went deeper into the glass, it would be considered carving. If the density were less than 100 percent, it would be considered shading.

Secondly, surface-etched glass has just two visual elements: the clear area and the etched area. The design can be thought of as black-and-white artwork in which all individual elements are separated from each other.

Finally, surface etching is done all at one time, or in a single stage. With carving and shading, where design elements touch, visual distinctions between elements can be created by a *multistage-blasting* process. With surface etching, since all elements are physically separated from each other in the design, they can be etched simultaneously.

Design for Surface Etching

Patterns for surface etching, like the completed etchings themselves, are limited to just two basic design elements (see the discussion of block designs in Chapter 4). When glass is etched, the surface becomes rough and you can no longer see through it. Glass which is etched with abrasives appears frosted and white, but because light still passes through, it is glowing and translucent rather than dull and opaque. The etched areas have not really changed from clear to white, but they appear that way because the roughened surface picks up and reflects ambient light rays from all angles. Although glass etched with etching cream appears grayer than glass etched with abrasives, the design still reads as positive and negative.

In contrast to the etched areas of glass, the unetched, or clear, areas seem relatively dark. This is because light rays pass right through clear glass. Whatever you see when you look at unetched glass is whatever is on the far side of the glass. Whether this is a tabletop (seen through a wine goblet or paperweight) or landscape (viewed

PROJECT: Positive Etch with Abrasive Blasting and Hand-Cut Resist

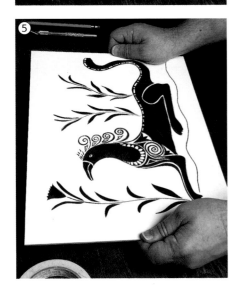

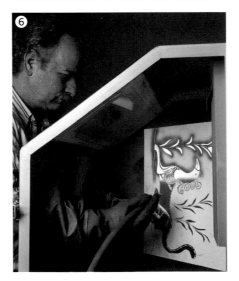

1 Apply the resist to the clean surface of the glass.

2 Prepare to transfer the design (here, with carbon paper).

3 Trace around each of the black elements to transfer the outline to the resist.

4 Cut each outline with your stencil knife. If the design is to be etched as a positive, as shown here, peel each element as it's cut. For a reverse etch, wait until all elements are cut, then peel off the background.

5 When all elements have been cut and peeled, the glass is ready to be etched.

6 Place the glass in the blasting cabinet. Move the nozzle back and forth, starting at the top of the glass and moving downward. Support the glass as you work. Note that the etched surface (which extends down to the back of the animal's head and behind the front leg) is bright, while the exposed, unetched glass appears very dark. (This photo shows the cabinet door open. Always blast with the door closed.)

7 Remove the resist and clean the glass thoroughly before mounting it in a frame·for display. Design by Ruth Dobbins, ©1997. Project patterns are included in the Appendix.

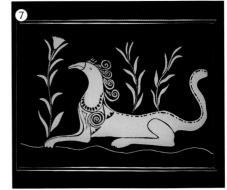

through a window or door panel), it will almost always be darker than the 'white' of the etched surface.

PLANNING ON PAPER

The fact that surface etching is composed of just two highly contrasting design elements should be considered as you choose or create a design. Plan and mark your design accordingly, so that you etch all elements you want to appear white, and leave unetched those elements that should appear dark.

In some cases, this is easier said than done. Because patterns are printed or drawn in dark ink or pencil on white paper, the original design tends to be black on a white background. However, the finished design usually appears as a white etching on a black background. The glass starts out clear, which reads visually as black, and the artist fills in the design elements with 'white.'

Black-on-White or White-on-Black?

If a design with a vine and flowers is printed in black on paper but etched in white on glass, the effect will be different, but not necessarily undesirable. However, if a design represents objects that are supposed to have distinct dark and light areas, you won't want to reverse them.

A design of a raccoon, for example, should show the distinctive black mask over a lighter colored face. If you don't plan the pattern carefully, the etched raccoon could have a white mask and look like a photographic negative. However, if you don't etch the mask at all, you'll encounter another problem. With no separation between the clear mask and the clear background, there will be nothing to define the edge of the raccoon's face in the area around the eyes. To solve this problem, modify the de-

Ruth Dobbins, *Nouveau*, surface-etched design on vase, 9H".

sign slightly by etching a line around the face. The outline will define the edge of the face without ruining the mask.

This kind of thoughtful planning is important when you use patterns from design books, as well as when you create your own designs. You'll confront the same sorts of problems with other black-and-white animals, any subject with a shadow, and many other kinds of designs.

DESIGN ORIENTATION

There's one more thing to keep in mind while creating or selecting a design. A piece of etched glass can be viewed from either the etched or the smooth side. The choice is usually based on personal preference and practicality, but it's an important consideration while you prepare your design, since a design etched on one side of the glass and viewed from the other will be reversed. This won't always cause a problem, but it will when lettering

is incorporated, or any other time when left-right orientation matters. If the design is to be viewed from the unetched (smooth) side of the glass, you must reverse it *before* transferring the design to the resist. It will happily reverse to the correct orientation when viewed from the smooth side.

Glass for Surface Etching

You can surface etch just about any type of glass. The most common projects for novice glass etchers are small to medium windows, and table pieces such as beer mugs or drinking glasses. These products are easy to etch, either by abrasive blasting or with an etching cream.

Rather than purchasing glass especially for etching, you may want to start your etching career with glass items that you already own. Look around: you may be surprised at how many candidates you have on hand. Glass tabletops, shelves and door panels, drinking glasses, wine goblets and serving bowls—all can be enhanced by etching. Once you've had some success, you'll want to purchase glass specifically for etching.

If you are just learning to etch, avoid abrasive etching on tempered glass; it will shatter if your blasting pressure is too high, your grit too coarse or your blasting time too long. Etching cream is a much better choice for beginners working with tempered glass.

Resists for Surface Etching

Whether you're blasting with abrasive or using etching cream, we recommend 4- to 8-mil opaque vinyl resist for your first surface-etching projects. Simply put, it's inexpensive and does a good job. If your design is relatively simple,

1. You need few tools and materials when working with etching cream: a stencil knife, towel, squeegee, masking tape, resist (not shown) and the object to be etched—here, a triangular bottle.

2. Fold the towel to support the sides of the bottle. Position the precut resist on the glass and tape one edge to create a hinge Use the hinge to turn the stencil upside down. Remove the backing paper to expose the adhesive.

3. Squeegee the resist down on the glass; avoid trapping air bubbles.

4. Remove the cover sheet. For a reverse etch like this one, the background resist is removed.

5. Tape the exposed glass surface and the edges of the glass, leaving a small wall of tape above the edge to keep the etching cream from spilling. Apply the cream per the manufacturer's instructions.

6. Wash off the etching cream under running water. Then remove the remaining tape and resist before a final cleaning.

7. Here's the finished piece. Design by Etchmaster Stencils, ©1997.

Ellen Abbott and Marc Leva, surface-etched and shaded sliding glass wall with appliquéd glass jewels, bevels and dichroic glass, corporate headquarters of Sulzer-Medica, Angleton, TX, photo: Paul Hester. This 18' x 9' wall is built in six panels. It features a soft, organic design created by the shading technique, contrasted with a highly graphic surface-etched background.

you might also try a 4- or 8-mil clear resist (not available in a 6-mil thickness), since you can place your pattern under the glass and cut the resist directly, without having to trace the pattern.

Once you've had a bit of experience, you may choose to use soft vinyl or rubber resists for surface etching. They're more expensive, but easier to cut. Base your choice on whether the extra expense is justified by the speed and ease of cutting. Hard vinyl resist can also work for surface etching three-dimensional glass so long as the object is straight-sided. Otherwise, you may have to use a softer, more stretchable resist like rubber or soft vinyl.

The quickest and easiest way to get started with glass etching is to use a precut stencil (suitable for

Paperweights of ½" plate glass, etched with stock photo-stencil designs.

abrasive etching or etching cream) or a photo resist (suitable only for abrasive etching). Since these require no enlarging of the design, no tracing and no cutting, you can produce an etching in very little time.

POSITIONING AND PEELING RESIST

You'll be applying the resist and transferring the design with one of the methods described in Chapter 4. But before you do, you'll need to decide whether you want a positive

Ruth and Norm Dobbins (design by Jamie Swift), surface-etched design on full-size tempered glass door panel, Swift residence.

Goddard & Gibbs Studio (London), John Lawson, door in private residence with surface-etched design produced by acid etching.

Ruth and Norm Dobbins, positive etched design with glue-chip textured background, part of a commercial product line, 9" x 18".

Joe Boron and Sandra Rodger, *Atomic Bowls* series, reverse surface-etched designs on glass bowls.

or negative (reverse) etching. A positive etching is one in which the main design elements are etched and the background is left clear. In a negative or reverse etching, the design is left clear and the background is etched.

This decision will affect not only the look of your etching, but also your cutting and peeling process. For a positive etch, peel each design element as it's cut; this makes the process easier by allowing you to see which elements have been cut and which haven't. For a reverse or negative etching, you'll have to cut around all design elements first, and then peel the background. In a complex design, you may want to mark an "X" in pencil through each line after you cut it, since it's sometimes difficult to see which lines have been cut.

Goddard & Gibbs Studio (London), John Lawson, pub window with surface-etched design produced by acid etching. This design shows various tones and textures that can be produced by acid etching.

Goddard & Gibbs Studio (London), John Lawson, pub window with surface-etched design produced by acid etching. This design shows various tones and textures that can be produced by acid etching.

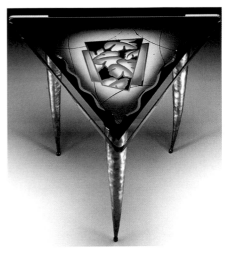

Joan Irving, *Triangle Table*, surface-etched tabletop with reverse-painted color in the etched areas, 20"H x 24" each side, photo: Ken West.

The Surface-Etching Process

When all is said and done, preparations for surface etching usually take longer than the etching itself. If you want to use abrasive etching, read the following section, which describes the procedure for that technique. If you don't own your own equipment, don't give up before you start! You can probably rent what you need from a nearby stained glass supply shop or equipment rental company.

If you want to start etching glass quickly and easily, without the expense of renting or purchasing equipment, try the etching creams that are available through hobby shops and stained glass suppliers. Skip ahead to the section on etching cream, later in this chapter.

ABRASIVE BLASTING

Once you've applied the resist to the glass, transferred and cut the design, and peeled the resist away from areas to be etched, you're ready to set up your equipment and blast.

You'll be working inside a *blast-*

Final Checks for Resist

After you've cut and peeled all elements, hold the glass up to a light source and check for little nubs at the edges of the cut lines. These nubs can occur when you accidently double-cut a line, or don't finish a cut in quite the same place that it started. Clean these up so the lines are straight and smooth.

At this point it's also wise to check for adhesive smudges on the exposed glass. Bits of adhesive can act as a resist, leaving unwanted clear spots on your design. These smudges can be cleaned off by rubbing with dry paper towel (and don't worry about scratching the glass—any scratches will be erased by the etching).

Murphy's Laws of Etching say that if adhesive is left on the glass during etching, you won't discover it until you have removed *all* the resist, at which point you can no longer correct it. However, if you discover these spots after you etch the glass, but *before* you remove the resist, you can usually reblast or reapply the etching cream. Sometimes slight irregularities remain.

PROJECT: Hand-Cut Stencil on Glass Mug

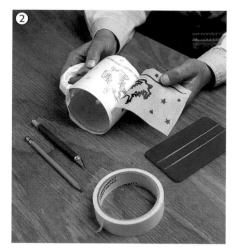

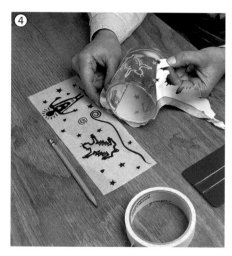

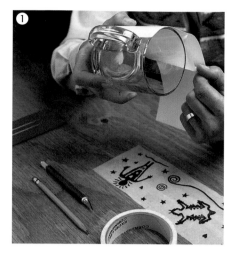

1. Cut rubber resist to size and adhere one edge next to the handle. As you pull off the backing paper, wrap the resist around the glass, pressing firmly.
2. Draw your design in soft black pencil, then tape it face down on the resist and transfer it by rubbing with the squeegee.
3. Cut out design with stencil knife; remove elements to be etched.
4. After etching with etching cream or by blasting, remove the resist for the final cleaning.
5. This finished mug shows the typical 'white' finish of abrasive blasting. *Vitroglyphs*™ series mug by Ruth Dobbins, ©1994.

ing cabinet, using either a *siphon blaster* or a *pressure blaster.* The cabinet contains the dust and abrasive during the blasting process, and a vacuum exhaust system attached to the cabinet extracts dust so you can see what you're doing while you work. This is not big, heavy-duty industrial equipment. An average unit takes up about the same space as a household washer or dryer, although it is taller—about five and a half feet tall. Smaller tabletop units can also be used, although they restrict the size of glass that can be etched.

Be sure to read the description of blasting equipment in Chapter 8, as well as the operating and safety information that accompanies the particular equipment you'll be using. Although the equipment is easy to use, it operates under pressure high enough to cause injury if not used in accordance with the manufacturer's instructions.

Before you start to blast, turn on your compressor and let it build up pressure. Meanwhile, fill the blaster with your chosen abrasive (see Chapter 8). If you are using a pressure blaster, turn on the main air valve to pressurize the blaster. Use the regulator to adjust the pressure to about 35 psi (pounds per square inch) for a pressure blaster, or about 80 psi for a siphon blaster.

Positioning the Glass

Place your glass in the cabinet, either on the easel (if you have one) or on the floor, leaning against the back. It's wise to have a perforated rubber mat in the cabinet to rest your glass on; this will keep it from being chipped or scratched on the metal of the cabinet. An inexpensive non-skid rubber mat—the kind you can pick up at a hardware store to use under a throw rug—works well for this purpose.

Close the cabinet door and turn on the light and vacuum system.

PROJECT: Found Resist on a Wine Glass

1 Cut-out vinyl stickers from hobby shops and office supply stores can serve as resist materials. In this case, we are applying stars to the cup portion of the wine glass, in preparation for a reverse etch.

2 The finished piece shows the clear stem and foot of the glass, which were covered with resist during the etching process.

Markian Olynyk and Brian Baxter, *2 Faces (2 Places)*, kiln-bent ¾" plate glass, surface etched using a liquid resist for texture, 84"H x 72"W x 22"D, photo: Joaquin Pedrero. The etched glass in this sculpture is bolted to steel plate which has a similar, etched texture.

Reach your hands in through the attached rubber gloves, pick up the nozzle (or gun, if using a siphon system), and you're ready to blast.

Blasting the Glass

It will be easiest to see what you're doing if the cabinet light is positioned so you can hold the glass in front of it while blasting, with the back of the cabinet somewhat in shadow and the glass brightly illuminated. The light source should be coming from your left if you are right-handed and vice versa if you are a lefty.

If the piece of glass is small enough to hold, pick it up with your free hand. If it's too large to hold, lean it against the back of the

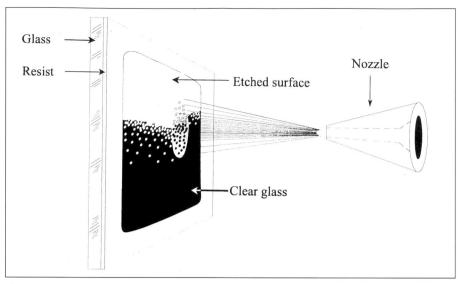

The density of the blast is greatest in the center of the area covered by the nozzle. Overlap each pass by 50 percent to achieve even coverage.

cabinet or an easel in the cabinet. Hold the nozzle perpendicular to the surface of the glass, from 6" to 8" away. This distance will create a spray width of about 1".

Step on the foot pedal (for a pressure blaster and some siphon guns) or pull the trigger (siphon gun only) to start the air-and-abrasive mixture shooting toward the glass. Begin with the nozzle pointed at the top of the piece and move your hand slowly back and forth while working your way down to the bottom. Cover all areas of the design evenly, overlapping your spray passes about 50 percent each time to ensure even coverage on the glass.

Julian and Karin Mesa, wood fence with surface-etched inserts of laminated safety glass, 4' x 4'.

The spray coming out of the nozzle is in a cone shape, and the density of the blast is strongest in the center, becoming lighter at the outside edges of the blasted area. Because of the lower concentration of abrasive at the edges of each pass, it's important to overlap passes 50 percent to achieve an even etch. If you don't, you'll have to go back over the etched surface several times to try to even it up.

Keep your nozzle at least 6" to 8" away from the surface of the glass; passes made at that distance are wide enough to make overlapping fairly easy. If the nozzle gets closer than 3", the blaster will actually gouge a groove in the glass.

Blasting Times

The length of time you need to spend blasting varies with the size of the area to be etched. Figure on moving your hand at about 1" per second across the surface of the glass, with the spray covering an area about 1" wide. Since you'll be overlapping each pass of the nozzle 50 percent over the prior pass, you'll move down the glass about

Ruth and Norm Dobbins, reverse surface-etched design with one stage of shading showing a gray tone, photo: Carolyn Wright.

REVERSE SURFACE ETCH ON IRIDIZED GLASS

1 The small piece of black iridized glass on the left shows the random color pattern on the surface. The larger piece has been blasted to remove the iridizing in the exposed areas, leaving a gray finish.

2 The finished piece has been sprayed with a clear lacquer to change the background from gray to black. The iridized pattern makes a striking contrast to the black background and frame.

REVERSE-ETCHED MIRROR BOX TOP

Reverse etching on the back of a mirror leaves the design mirrored and the background with a white satin finish.

ETCHED BEVELED-GLASS BOX TOP

A positive etched design on the back surface of the glass shows up well. Boxes like this one are available from stained glass suppliers.

$1/2$" with each pass. Generally, you can assume that a monogram on a glass mug will take about fifteen seconds if the letters are 2" high. A 12" x 12" flat glass panel for a window or door will take about five minutes.

Your goal with surface etching is to blast until all exposed glass has an even white finish. If you continue beyond this point, you'll be carving rather than surface etching, and should refer to Chapter 6 for information on that technique.

Once you think you've etched the exposed areas of glass evenly, turn off the blaster and set the glass down in the cabinet. Wait just a minute for the vacuum to clear out the dust before opening the cabinet to remove the glass. Dust the piece and hold it up to a light source to see if there are any blank spots, skips or streaks in the etching. If there are, take a pencil or marker and circle the areas which need more blasting. Continue blasting until these marks disappear—and the blank spots along with them.

ETCHING WITH CREAM

If you are using etching cream instead of blasting, apply the cream to the design areas on the glass according to the manufacturer's instructions. Each manufacturer has different recommended procedures; follow them carefully to get an even etch over the entire surface. Some of the creams etch in only two or three minutes, but need to be constantly 'stirred' while on the glass. Others take eight to ten minutes, but do not require stirring.

When applying etching cream to curved surfaces, make sure your application is not so heavy that it runs off the glass and onto the table surface; if necessary, make a small dam of masking tape or resist

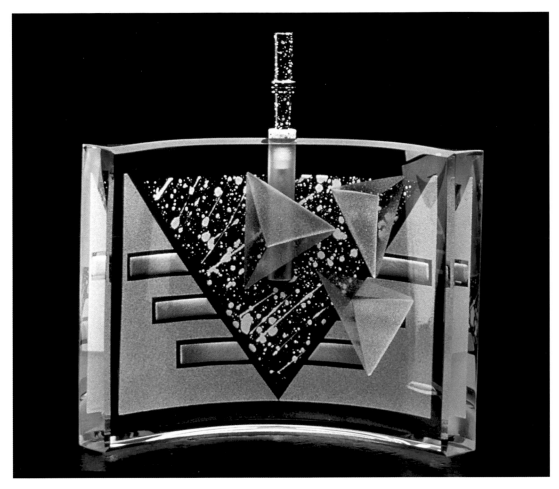

Joan Irving, *Iriad*, 3/4" slumped glass, multistage blasted with reverse painting, core-drilled, aluminum stopper. Surface-etched elements echo the background shapes.

all around the design. Most etching creams are fairly thick and will not run excessively unless applied in a very heavy coating.

When the etching is finished, clean or wash off the cream according to instructions. Wipe the glass dry.

FINISHING THE PROJECT

While the resist is still on the glass, check to be sure that all etching cream or abrasive particles have been removed. Traces of these substances can scratch or etch the clear surface as you peel off the resist.

Work carefully and gently when removing the resist, and rest your glass piece flat on the work surface. Start at one corner and pull straight back across the glass. If you pull too hard or if you pull straight up while removing the resist, you could snap the glass. After removing the resist, clean off any remaining fingerprints or adhesive remaining on the glass.

Now you can admire your work! (No instructions necessary.)

6

Carving

Carving offers a more realistic looking—and to many eyes, more beautiful—approach to glass etching. Carved designs are actually three-dimensional, in contrast to those created by surface etching. Elements in a carved design can also touch each other; they need not be separated by 'artificial' clear spaces as required in surface etching. Carved elements can touch because they are blasted to different depths along their common edges. These distinctions are readily visible, and have the effect of clearly defining design elements.

Since carving allows these additional possibilities, it inspires the creation of much more sophisticated glass etchings. Of course, as the level of sophistication increases, so does the amount of time required both to master techniques and to finish an individual piece.

Carving Perspective

Because glass is transparent, carving requires a most interesting shift in perspective on the part of the artist. Carved flat glass almost always looks better when viewed from the smooth, uncarved side; indeed, most carvings are *designed* to be viewed from this side. (The primary exception is carving on glassware—which is almost always

Wendy Saxon-Brown, *Lady with Leopard on a Couch*, multistage-carved plate glass, etched on both sides, with applied color, 27" x 17".

Kathy Barnard, *Nasturtium*, dining set and tabletop, lightly carved and surface etched, sterling flatware by Robyn Nichols.

done on the outside.) For this reason, the artist must work from the back of the glass—the second surface—carving a negative or hollow shape that will appear as a positive to the viewer.

When carving, the artist must not only be able to visualize the three-dimensional object or scene he wishes to create, but also have complete control of the blasting process necessary to create the form. With enough practice, a carver can look at a black-and-white line drawing and visualize the design not just in three-dimensions, but also in reverse—and know exactly how to create the shape of each element in the design.

At least this is the goal. In reality, it takes years of experience to reach this point. The novice carver should not despair, however, as even the simplest carving projects can be very beautiful. Furthermore, with the approach described in this chapter, the beginner can quickly achieve success and begin to learn the process of reverse visualization.

Visual Effects

There are four variables that the glass carver must understand and be able to control before he can achieve good quality carvings.

Type of carving—either uniform or variable depth—used in each design element.

Depth of relief—shallow, medium or deep—of each element and of the carving as a whole.

Carving perspective—either bas-relief (a positive shape on the first surface) or reverse bas-relief (a negative or hollow shape on the second surface, to be viewed from the opposite side).

Degree of contrast with the background, ranging from high contrast (with a clear background) to low contrast (with an etched background).

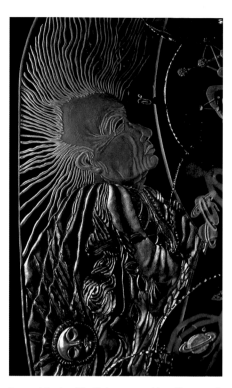

Raquel Stolarski, *Clairvoyants* (detail), carved plate glass, hand painted, mixed media, 31½" x 65¾" x 19¾".

Char Vowell, *House*, carved plate glass assemblage with kiln-formed glass accents and reverse-painted highlights, ½" thick base, 9½" x 5" x 5".

The Carving Process: An Overview

Because of the need to accurately create the three-dimensional shape or contour of each element—including the shape and angle of the sidewalls—carving requires a greater degree of control than surface etching. This control is achieved by manipulating the distance of the nozzle from the glass, the angle of the nozzle to the glass, and the speed of your hand motion—all at the same time. Of course, you must be able to do these things while looking through the virtual dust storm you are creating in your blasting cabinet.

Carving also requires a different hand motion than surface etching. In surface etching, you move the nozzle back and forth across the surface of the glass, overlapping passes by 50 percent at a distance of 6" to 8". Your goal is to blast until the exposed surface is uniformly white.

When carving, blast elements separately, one at a time. Follow the basic outline of each element, and move in a continuous spiral, inward to the center of the element and then out again to the perimeter, until you achieve the desired contour and depth. Spend more time in areas that need to be deeper, and less in shallow areas of the design. Passes should overlap about 75 percent in order to control the evenness of the carving, and the distance from the nozzle to the glass should normally range from about 1" to 6". In all, carving a given design can take up to ten times longer than surface etching the same design.

Glass Choices for Carving

The most common flat glass used for carving is ¼" plate. It's accessible and relatively inexpensive; it's also thick enough to carve to visibly distinct depths. Thicker glass—³⁄₈", ½" or ¾"—can be used in projects calling for increased strength or dramatic effect. Even on heavy plate glass, most carving is not deeper than ⅛". Indeed, most carved designs average ¹⁄₁₆" to ³⁄₃₂" deep.

Of course, it is possible to cut deeper—even all the way through the glass for certain visual effects—but do so with caution. Deep carving can weaken glass enough to cause a window or door panel to shatter with exposure to strong winds or slamming. Consult with an experienced plate glass installer if you have any questions about adequate thickness of glass for architectural installations.

Almost any type of three-dimensional glass can be carved, so long as it's thick enough to maintain its strength after carving. As a general rule, you shouldn't carve glass less than $3/16$" thick. Again, the depth of your carving should be dictated by aesthetics, use and safety. If you carve too deeply, and the glass is exposed to rough handling or significant temperature changes (as in a dishwasher or strong sunlight), it may crack.

Carving on safety glass requires special planning, and tempered safety glass should not be carved at all; please see the discussion in Chapter 2. With tableware, you must be on the lookout for tempered glass, which is sometimes used to make cups, mugs and dinner plates. Be sure to ask about any glassware you intend to carve before purchasing it.

Resists for Carving

Because carving erodes greater quantities of glass than surface etching, it requires much longer blasting times. Longer blasting subjects the resist to additional wear and tear from the abrasive, as well as overheating from friction gener-

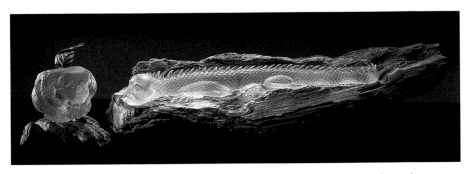

Barry Sautner, *Lusting the Freshly Fallen Fruit*, glass carved in full relief, petrified wood, malachite. 4"H x 26"W x 5"D, photo: Douglas Schaible.

Julian and Karin Mesa, *Audubon Osprey With Feather Border*, multistage-carved and shaded ½" plate glass, wooden stand, 42" x 84", photo: Cory Byrne.

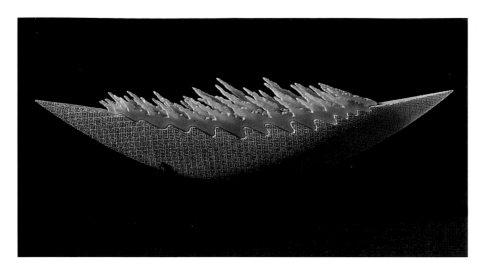

William LeQuier, *Headdress*, laminated, carved and wheel-cut ³/₈" plate glass, 32"L x 12"H x 2¹/₄"D, photo: Gerard Roy.

ated during blasting. Both conditions increase the chances that the resist will fail. It's important to compensate by 1) using a thicker, tougher resist, 2) moving the nozzle over the resist more quickly, 3) holding the nozzle further from the glass, and/or 4) lowering the blasting pressure.

Typically, a 12- to 25-mil soft vinyl or rubber resist is used for glass carving. These pliable materials can absorb more blasting force than hard vinyl resists. They are also better able to dissipate the heat generated from the friction of the abrasive particles, though it's still important to keep the nozzle moving. If the nozzle is left in one spot too long, the heat can actually melt or burn the resist.

WORKING WITH SOFT RESISTS

Rubber and soft vinyl resists feel soft and pliable, a little like pizza dough. That's a good thing to keep in mind when applying them to glass, since they can stretch out of shape if pulled too hard.

Cut the resist about a half inch larger in each dimension than the glass it will cover. Apply by pulling

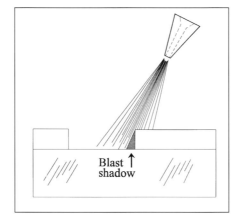

a couple of inches of backing paper away from the resist along one edge. Crease the paper and attach the exposed resist. On small pieces, use your thumb to press the resist down along the edge first, then smooth it across the rest of the surface with your thumb or fingers. On larger pieces, use a squeegee to apply the resist, after first adhering it to the edge of the glass. Be sure not to *push* the squeegee across the resist surface, but rather turn it over and pull it. To avoid trapping air bubbles, always pull from the edge where the resist is attached toward the opposite edge.

After the resist is attached, trim

it flush with the edge of the glass and check for air bubbles. Go slow and easy if you need to lift the resist to get rid of air bubbles; you can make things worse if you stretch the resist as you pull it. If all else fails, puncture the bubbles and patch with more resist.

FINE LINES AND BLAST SHADOW

It *is* possible to use the thinner vinyls if you need to carve very fine detail. Since these resists are less durable, you'll need to compensate by lowering blasting pressure and limiting the abrasive flow. We use 4- or 6-mil hard vinyl when we're carving intricate designs or geometric patterns with narrow parallel lines and precise angles.

By using these thinner resists, you can also avoid a phenomenon called *blast shadow*. When you use a resist 18 mils thick or more, you should hold your nozzle at right angles to the glass while blasting. If you allow the nozzle to blast at an oblique angle for any length of time, the carving may not extend all the way up to the edge of the element. This is caused by the edges of the element being in the 'shadow' cast by the thick resist.

Carving Styles

There are three major carving styles—single-stage, two-stage and multistage—and each requires a different approach to removing the resist and blasting. A piece of carved glass can incorporate one, two or all three styles depending on the complexity of the design.

SINGLE-STAGE CARVING

In surface etching, you work with block designs and blast all elements at one time, sweeping your nozzle across the whole expanse of exposed glass. In single-stage carving, you also use block designs, but you blast more deeply. In addition, you blast just one element at a time, carving it to the desired depth before moving on to other elements. Instead of just blasting the surface of the glass, you'll blast for a much longer time, until the glass is deeply eroded. Thus, although the initial design looks the same as a surface-etching design, the finished piece is distinctly different, with the design clearly sculpted into the glass. It's a richer, three-dimensional effect.

Ruth Dobbins, *Sun Warrior*, slumped 1/4" plate glass, single-stage carved from the front of the glass, gilded, 16"H x 12"W, photo: Carolyn Wright.

Two-Stage Carving

In two-stage carving, you carve the glass to two different depths to create distinctions between design elements that touch. To do this, you need a line drawing instead of a block design.

The most common type of two-stage carving is called *outlining*. Imagine a design of a flower and leaves, with a narrow double outline around the perimeter of each petal. Resist between the double outline is removed (a parallel line cutter makes this easy), and the outline is blasted evenly and fairly deeply. Next, resist is removed from the inside of each element and the design is blasted again—this time quite lightly. Voilà, you have a two-stage carving.

In another form of two-stage carving, adjoining elements are blasted to alternating depths, as with a flower where every other petal is either deep or shallow. (Be sure to have an even number of petals if you experiment with this kind of design.) The effect of two-stage carving is somewhat more realistic than single-stage, although still fairly stylized. The only way to achieve a natural, three-dimensional look is with multistage carving.

Multistage Carving

There are two primary things to learn with multistage carving. First, you must be able to determine the correct blasting sequence for the elements in your design. We'll explain how to do this through a process of analyzing and numbering design elements based on how they overlap. Second, and just as important, you need to be able to create the correct shape of each element as you blast by manipulating a number of physical variables: pressure setting, abrasive flow, angle and distance of the nozzle in relation to the glass, and the speed at which you move the nozzle.

Establishing the Blasting Sequence

By establishing the correct blasting sequence, you'll create a design that looks 'right'—that is, the ele-

A block design, suitable for single-stage carving.

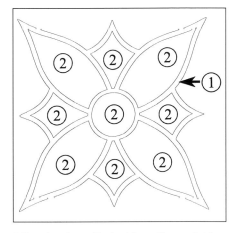

A line drawing with double outline, suitable for two-stage carving.

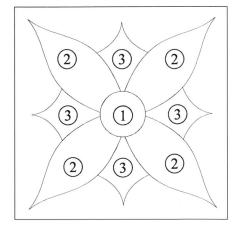

A line drawing, suitable for multistage carving.

ments are in the correct relationship to each other. In addition, your analysis will show you when it's possible to blast several elements during the same stage without losing correct spatial relationships. This can be a significant time saver.

Most glass carving is done as a reverse bas-relief from the second surface of the glass. It's not always easy to visualize the steps in carving this kind of project—especially in the beginning—but don't despair. The process used to determine the blasting sequence is quite simple. Stay with us, and you'll quickly grasp the concept.

The goal of your analysis is to assign a number to each element,

Ruth Dobbins, *Flower-Star*, rosewood box carved in three stages with lightly shaded center, 1/4" beveled glass, 5"Dia.

J.D. Francis, carved plate glass booth divider (detail), design by Randy Calm, 20" x 30". The top edge of this piece has been carved with the blaster.

identifying the blasting stage for that particular element. Any element marked #1 is blasted in the first round, or stage, of blasting. All elements marked #2 are blasted in the second stage, etc. Any number of elements can have the same stage number, as long as they don't touch, and as long as they're in the correct sequence.

You'll determine the correct number for each element through a series of questions about what we call the *overlap sequence*. Take a look at the design of three overlapping Gingko leaves on the following page. Because the leaves overlap, there are seven separate and distinct visual elements, randomly labeled C, M, R, L, Y, P and A.

As you go through the following analysis, write the sequence numbers on your paper pattern rather than on—or in addition to—the resist. Otherwise, you'll lose track of the numbers as you peel the resist, and have to renumber if you want to carve the design again.

Wally Zampa, *Phoenix*, multistage-carved plate glass, 20" x 60", photo: Jeff Teeter.

Nathan Allan Glass Studios, interior glass panels, carved, curved, frosted and lacquered.

The Stage-Numbering Process

1. Pick any element in the design as a starting point. Let's pick R. Focus your attention on R and ask: *What unnumbered elements does this element touch?* The answer is C, P, M and A.

2. Ask this question: *Where these unnumbered elements touch R, which one is on top, R or one of the others?* If R is on top, stay focused on it. Otherwise, shift your attention to the one you found to be on top.

In this case, when you compare R to C, you see that R is on top of C. R is also on top of P and A. But when you compare R to M, you see that M overlaps R. Since this is the case, shift your attention to M and temporarily forget the others. It doesn't matter if there are several elements on top of the one you are focused upon initially. Just shift your attention to the first one you find.

3. Now, with your focus on M, identify the unnumbered elements that touch it. They are R,

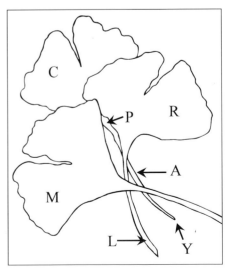

A simple carving design, ready to number for stage blasting.

P, C, A, Y and L. When you compare these to M, one at a time, you'll find that M is on top of all of them. An element that is on top of all others is blasted in the first stage, so start numbering by assigning M the number '1.'

To move through this process most efficiently, compare each element to the one on which you are focused as soon as you determine that they touch. Thus, instead of first identifying all unnumbered elements that also touch M, and *then* comparing them, just compare them one at a time as you identify them.

4 Start with any unnumbered element that touches your #1 element and repeat step 2. Let's pick C and go through the questioning process:

What unnumbered element touches C? R does.

Which is on top, R or C? R is, so temporarily forget C and focus on R.

What unnumbered elements touch R and which one is on top?

Savoy Studios, sculpture for the ship *Splendour of the Sea*, Royal Caribbean Cruise Line, edge lit with fiber optics, 10'H x 3'Dia. Design and carved figures: Sue Grauten; building image: Dan Woodward; etching on buildings: Rich Lamothe and Melissa Andrews.

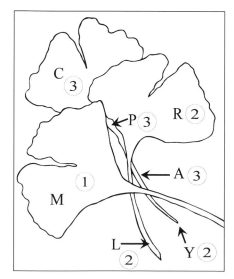

Stage numbers have been assigned. Note there is one element in the #1 stage, three elements in the #2 stage, and three elements in the #3 stage.

A does, and R is on top of A, so keep your focus on R.

What other unnumbered elements touch R and which one is on top? P does, and R is on top, so keep your focus on R.

What other unnumbered elements touch R and which one is on top? C does, and R is on top; keep your focus on R. No other unnumbered elements touch R.

Since R is on top of all the unnumbered elements that it touches, it is now R's turn to be assigned a number. *What number should it be?* It must be one number higher than the highest number it touches. It touches a #1, so it should be assigned #2.

5 Move your focus to any unnumbered element that touches any numbered element. Let's try P. It touches not one but two numbered elements. Since it doesn't

touch any other unnumbered elements, P can be numbered without further analysis. Its number is 3, one number higher than the highest numbered element it touches.

6 Move your focus to the other unnumbered elements. You'll see that A and C are #3's, while Y and L are #2's.

7 Once all design elements are numbered, check any elements which have the same number. This is fine, so long as the elements don't touch! If they do, assign a higher number to the element which is 'below' its neighbor.

Numbering a Regular Bas-Relief

If you are carving on the front surface of a piece of glass, the carving will be a regular bas-relief. Just reverse the process described above so that top elements are carved last, instead of first.

The most important thing you can accomplish by the stage-numbering process is to ensure that top elements are blasted more deeply than their neighbors *along the edge where they touch*. As an added benefit of this process, you'll be able to remove resist for all elements with the same number at the same time. Even though you'll blast the elements separately, it will still save a considerable amount of time to peel the resist from like-numbered elements and blast them all in one operation, as opposed to removing the glass from the blasting cabinet over and over again to remove each piece of resist separately.

Trace or copy the pattern at right and try using the stage-numbering process to number the elements. Turn the page to see the same design with a correct sequence of numbers. With a little experience, you should be able to number a moderately complex design in just a few minutes. Practice on any line drawing, whether or not you intend to carve it.

Stage and Depth

Don't confuse stage numbers with the depth to which you should carve each element. In other words, all #1 elements will not necessarily be the same depth, nor will #2's, etc. The depth to which you should carve each element is determined by the perspective of the design. In our example, Y is the stem of leaf C, which is further from the viewer than leaf M and leaf R. Although R and Y are both #2 elements, R will be blasted deeper than Y because it is closer to the viewer in the design. Of

Practice numbering this design, then check the numbered version on page 89.

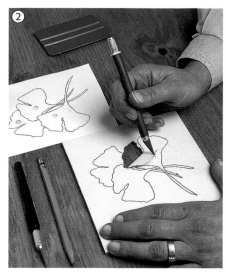

1 With a pencil drawing and rubber resist, the best way to transfer the design is to position it face down on the resist and rub (burnish) it with a squeegee.

2 After cutting the entire design with the stencil knife, remove the resist from all stage #1 elements and blast.

3 Check the depth of carving on stage #1 elements before removing and blasting stage #2 elements. In a simple pattern like this, your depth should be about one-third the thickness of the glass.

4 With stage #2 elements carved, stage #3 elements are removed. Note the highlights and shadows at the edges of the resist, showing the depth of carving.

5 Examine the carved elements for depth and surface contour before removing the rest of the resist. Check the glass from the back to see how deeply you've carved.

6 After determining that no further blasting or touch-ups are necessary, remove the last resist and clean the piece.

7 The completed etching.

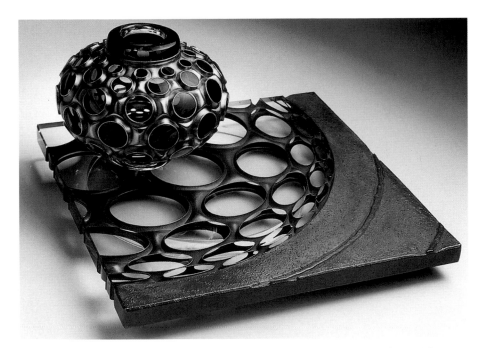

Michael Glancey, *Fundamental Dominion*, blown glass vase, deeply carved on the outside surface, mounted on a carved ³/₄" plate-glass base, copper coloration, 6¹/₂"H x 12"W x 12"D.

course, the deeper you carve into the back of the glass, the closer the element will appear when the glass is turned around. In a complex design with dozens or hundreds of elements, it is common for elements of widely varying numbers to be the same depth and elements of the same number to be carved to widely varying depths.

BLASTING VARIABLES

Before you can carve successfully, you need to understand the variables in the physical blasting setup. These include the size of the nozzle, the pressure at which you need to blast, the distance of the nozzle from the glass, the speed of hand motion over the glass, the abrasive setting, and the angle of the nozzle to the surface of the glass. All these variables interact with each other, and you can't change one without affecting all the rest.

The pressure you use will depend on the size of the element

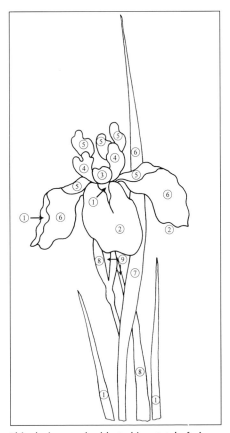

This design can be blasted in a total of nine stages.

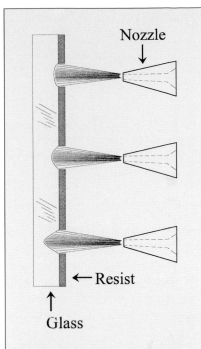

Blasting for a longer time allows the abrasive to cut into the glass more deeply. Note that as the cut gets deeper, it changes from a shallow U-shape to a deeper V-shape.

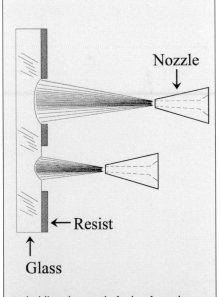

By holding the nozzle farther from the glass, you'll etch a wider area that's more gradual and less steep. This makes it easier to carve to a smoother, even depth. By holding the nozzle closer, you'll produce a narrower, steeper shape, and cut more quickly.

you're carving and the speed at which you want to carve. You should blast from a distance that allows the spray to cover about one-third to one-half the width of the element you're blasting, with a maximum coverage of about 1". Your goal is a smooth, evenly carved surface. The smaller the element, the closer you can hold the nozzle to the glass, but beware! By moving closer, you'll not only cut into the glass faster, but also wear out the resist more quickly. If the nozzle is *too* close, you may cause the resist to come off, or blast all the way through the glass. In addition, when you carve too fast you have less control over the shape you are creating. As a general rule of thumb, whenever you move the nozzle closer to the glass, compensate by reducing the blasting pressure.

The opposite is also true: the larger the elements, the farther away you'll need to hold the nozzle, up to a maximum of about 8". With a $3/32$" diameter nozzle (the average nozzle size on pressure blasters), an 8" distance will give you a spray width of about an inch. The greater distance will yield a smoother and more evenly carved area, but your blasting speed will be slowed considerably. You can compensate by raising the pressure.

It's not unusual to adjust blasting pressure and speed many times while working on one pattern to accommodate elements of various sizes. Just to make things more interesting, you can also affect the speed of carving and smoothness of the surface contour by moving the nozzle over the glass more or less quickly. Keep in mind that a contour that varies drastically in depth (as opposed to an even, smooth contour) is sometimes desirable, so you need to know how to produce it.

Barbara Boeck, free-standing divider panel (detail), $1/2$" laminated plate glass, 18" x 85", private residence. The artist used free-hand carving within elements to shape facial contours.

Below: Deborah Goldhaft, *Whale and Salmon*, tabletop, multistage carving on both sides of $1/4$" mirror and on one side of $1/4$" plate glass (top layer), 49" x 28", photo: Michael Rosenberg.

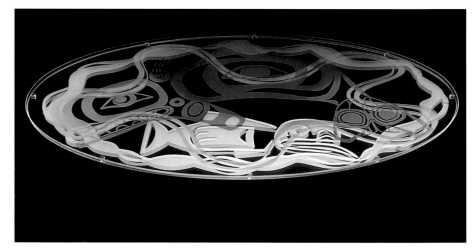

Novice carvers tend to want absolute, fixed limits regarding these variables. Because so many factors interconnect, that's just not possible. Successful carvers develop a keen ability to see what's happening on the surface of the glass, and make many small adjustments as they carve. Eventually, their inner dialog sounds something like this:

"Move more quickly over this area ... now pull the nozzle a little farther back ... now closer and slow down to carve a deep groove ... now faster ... oops! That area is getting too deep, avoid it from now on ..." and so forth, all in a matter of a few seconds. The whole process is fluid and dynamic, and practice is the key to success.

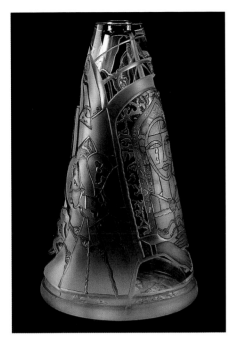

Bernice Ferman, *Rites of Passage*, carved blown glass with applied color.

For the sample carving projects in this chapter, as well as most others with elements of similar size, the average blasting pressure will be from 20 to 40 psi (pounds per square inch) with a pressure blaster, or 60 to 90 psi with a siphon blaster. The distance from the nozzle to the glass will vary between 1" and 6", and the speed at which you should move the nozzle will be about 1/2" to 2" per second.

The Carving Process

Once you've numbered your pattern, you're ready to peel the resist and blast. With single-stage carving, remove resist for all elements to be blasted. For two-stage and multistage projects, remove the re-

sist on all #1 elements only. You'll be blasting them one at a time before moving on to #2 elements.

Before you start blasting, take a moment to think about the depth and contour of each element. You may even want to make notes on the pattern. When you know how you want to proceed, place the glass into the blasting cabinet and pressurize the blaster.

BLASTING

With single-stage carving, you'll blast all elements in the same stage, though one at a time. With two-stage and multistage projects, peel the elements in their correct stage, but still carve one element at a time. Start at the outside of the element and move the nozzle around

The Physical Variables of Carving

VARIABLE	CONDITION OR ACTION	EFFECT
Air pressure	higher pressure	cuts the glass faster
	lower pressure	opposite effect
Nozzle size	larger	wider spray pattern
	smaller	opposite effect
Distance from nozzle to glass	closer	narrower spray pattern; abrasive cuts the glass faster
	farther	opposite effect
Speed of moving the nozzle over the glass	slower	cuts into the glass more deeply with each pass; cuts a slightly wider area
	faster	opposite effect
Angle of nozzle to glass		determines the shape of the cut into the glass
Abrasive setting (only possible with pressure blasters)	high concentration of abrasive in the air stream	faster carving
	lower concentration of abrasive in the air stream	slower carving

the perimeter. Working at a constant distance from the glass, slowly bring the nozzle to the center of the element and then back to the perimeter again, always working in a spiral path. To carve to an even depth, move your hand at a consistent speed and overlap each pass of the nozzle about 75 percent over the prior pass. In most cases, you'll want to keep the nozzle perpendicular to the surface of the glass; otherwise, you'll get unintentional undercuts or other carved shapes you may not want.

As you get comfortable with the process, you'll find that you can carve certain shapes better by holding the nozzle at an angle. For example, you can undercut scales on a fish or dragon to make them look more dramatic and three-dimensional. (The drawings on this and the following pages illustrate this and other advanced techniques.)

Keep the shape of the element you want to create in mind while you work. For a convex shape (when viewed from the opposite side of the glass), concentrate the blast in the center of the element rather than the outside edges. For a concave shape, do the opposite. If

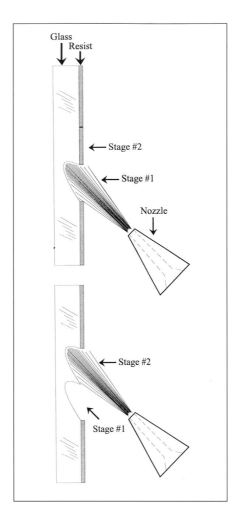

De Carter-Hoffman, *From Me to Thee*, recognition piece, multistage carving on cut and polished ³/₄" glass, 16³/₄" x 8" x 8".

the element has an undulating contour, concentrate the blast on areas which should be closest to the viewer, and vary the distance of the nozzle to the glass. Move the nozzle closer to the glass when blasting a smaller area, and further away for a wider carved area. Once you have achieved sufficient depth and the desired shape in one element, move on to the next, until all #1 elements have been blasted.

Stop blasting and give the vacuum exhaust a chance to clear the dust out of the cabinet. Remove the glass and brush the loose dust from both sides (an inexpensive 3" paintbrush is good for this). Check the depth and contour of the #1 elements for areas that need additional blasting. If necessary, return the

glass to the cabinet and continue shaping the #1 elements. Once these are completed to your satisfaction, remove the resist from the #2 elements and continue.

WHEN DESIGN ELEMENTS TOUCH

Where elements touch, you'll need to work with utmost care. Your goal is to keep the distinct shape of the first element while still creating enough depth in the second element so that it looks 'normal' in relationship to the first. If the first shape is deep overall, and the second shape is too shallow, the elements will not look like they belong together. It's important to create adequate depth in the second element while keeping a sharp edge between the two elements. Blasting for too long, close to the edge between the elements, blurs the edge and ruins the distinction.

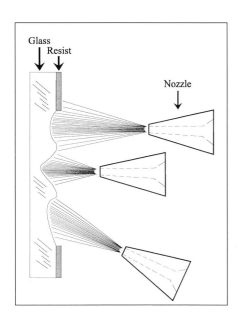

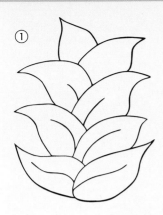

① A *disappearing line* is a line that stops in the middle of an element without touching another line. They are essential to realism in representational designs, and are common in intermediate and advanced patterns. Take the time to learn this technique.

1 There are six disappearing lines in this pattern. Continue each with a dotted line until it reaches another line. The dotted line shows where you will cut with your stencil knife, but the dotted line will not show in the finished piece. You have now made each leaf that has a disappearing line into two separate elements.

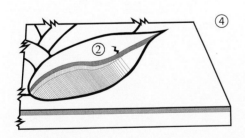

Resist →
Glass →

2 Draw a zigzag line across the point where the disappearing line stops and the dotted line starts. Number each element separately, according to the usual stage-numbering rule. Because the leaves with disappearing lines are now two separate elements, each must have its own number. In each case, the lower half appears in front of the upper half, and has a lower number to indicate that fact.

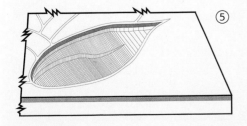

3 To show the process of carving each leaf, we have enlarged a section of the pattern as it appears on the glass. We will be showing only one leaf, but the others should be carved in the same way.

4 Remove the resist from the element with the lower number. Blast the portion of that element surrounded by the solid line, but completely avoid the portion where the dotted line is. Also avoid the portion of the solid line that is close to the dotted line because the overspray will inevitably hit the dotted line and carve into the glass in that area. (When you remove the resist from the first half and start blasting, you will quickly lose track of the place where the solid line stops and the dotted line starts. That's the reason for the zigzag line—to show where to stop blasting.) The carving should be deeper at the base of the leaf and shallower as it approaches the point where the line disappears.

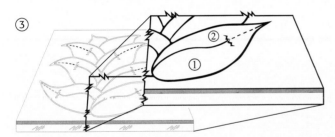

5 Remove the resist from the second half of the element. Carve the second half completely, all the way up to the point of the leaf and around the point back down into the first half. Blend the two together from the point back to where the line disappears. Since there was no depth carved along the dotted line when the first half of the leaf was exposed, the line disappears, as shown.

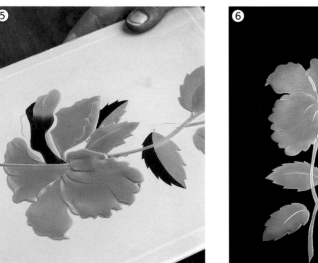

1 Transfer the pattern to the rubber resist by burnishing it with a squeegee.

2 After cutting the pattern, remove all stage #1 elements. With a complex pattern, there can be many elements with the same number.

3 When all #1 elements are blasted to depth, remove the #2 elements and blast.

4 Continue the process through the rest of the stages.

5 Check your progress frequently from the smooth side of the glass.

6 The finished piece. Note the disappearing lines and undercut elements.

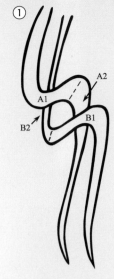

Interwoven elements are common in designs that illustrate, for example, vines, latticework, or the mane of a horse. Because elements are both above and beneath each other at different points, they seem to present an impossible situation for numbering and blasting, but there *is* a solution.

1 In the example shown here, elements A and B have each been divided into two separate elements with a dotted line. These 'artificial' cut lines are not on the original pattern and will not show up in the finished piece. They are placed approximately halfway between the 'high' and 'low' points of the element (the points at which it's on top of—and below—its neighbor).

Peel and blast the #1 portion of each element, carving most deeply in the area that overlaps the neighboring element. The carving should be increasingly shallow the closer it gets to the artificial cut line, with no carving whatsoever at the line.

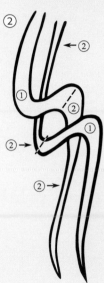

2 Now peel the second half of the split elements. Blend the two halves together by carving the second half to match the depth created in the first half. Because no depth was carved into the glass at the artificial cut line when the first half was blasted, the transition from one half to the other will be seamless.

Before beginning your first carving project, it's a good idea to practice blasting adjoining elements on scrap glass. Check with your local plate glass shops for free or low-cost scraps. Most shops throw away pieces of glass larger than you'll need for many projects.

Experimenting will teach you a lot about carving. If you move faster in certain spots than others, the carving will give you away by being shallower in these areas. If you always change directions in the same spot, and don't move on to the resist while doing so, you will create a depression at the point of change. We call these *craters*, and they are just about impossible to get rid of.

There's something magical about carving glass, about watching this hard, brittle material melt away under the force of the blaster. Remember that it's a dynamic process. You'll learn much more—and learn it more quickly—by practicing as much as you can. The eye-hand coordination necessary for glass carving cannot be learned by reading, only by doing.

A final note. Some processes are best explained through illustration—including the techniques used to create disappearing lines and interwoven elements. Although these processes are illustrated in this chapter, the same techniques are used with shading, which is the subject of the following chapter.

7

Shading

Shading is the last of the three primary abrasive-etching techniques. Although it is the least well-known and least understood of the techniques, it can be used to produce some of the most delicate and elegant results. Shaded etching resembles airbrushing, both in look and in the method of creation, and is the only way to produce apparent shades of gray in a piece of etched glass. It is striking not only when used alone, but also in combination with other etching techniques.

Shading, like carving, is a multi-stage technique. This means that distinctions between elements are not created by artificial separations as with surface etching, but rather by blasting each element to a different extent than other elements that touch it. With carving, an element that is blasted to a greater extent (for a longer time or at a higher pressure or both) is carved more deeply. In shading, blasting to a greater extent means creating a whiter finish in the etched area, while blasting to a lesser extent means leaving the etched area grayer. Thus, the distinguishing factor among shaded elements is the shade of gray, on a scale from black to white.

Interestingly, few glass etchers ever learn the shading technique. There are several reasons for this.

Barry Hood, *Shining Mountain Woman*, 28" x 42", photo: Tim Rice. Notice the double reverse shading: the figure is virtually unblasted against the light background landscape, while the hands, earrings, necklace and smaller landscape are shaded in positive against the dark background of the body. The tree line in front of the small landscape is reversed as well.

Ellen Abbott and Marc Leva, *Winter*, 18" x 18". This panel includes carved details in the cut-crystal vase, fruit and pine cones. Shading is used to represent their darker, softer reflections.

essary control, the technique can be intimidating to learn.

Although shading can take longer to learn than carving, a shaded piece can be completed much more quickly than a carved piece of equal complexity. This is simply because it takes less time to lightly etch each element than to carve those same elements deeply into the glass.

Principles of Shaded Etching

- Shading is a multistage technique.
- It can be done on any type or thickness of glass.
- The distinctions between elements are created by contrasting shades of gray wherever one element touches another.
- Clear, unetched glass surfaces appear dark or black. Surfaces that are etched 100 percent appear light or white. Surfaces etched with a density between zero and 100 percent appear as shades of gray.
- For best contrast, a shaded design should be viewed against a dark background.
- Shaded etchings show up well when viewed from near or far, and designs can be realistic and delicate. In contrast, surface-etched pieces show up well at any distance, but are not very realistic or delicate. Carved pieces can be realistic and delicate, but show up poorly from distances over 20 feet.

First, the technique itself has not been widely practiced and is not well-known. Many people who have been etching for years either don't know about shading, or don't understand how it's accomplished.

Second, the blasting technique used to produce shaded effects seems to contradict the logic of the techniques used for surface etching and carving; because of this, the process may seem counterintuitive. With surface etching and carving, you learn to blast the exposed surface of the glass completely and evenly to get a high-quality result. In contrast, shading requires you to blast only selected areas of each element, and to do so with uneven, but controlled, coverage of the surface. This can be both confusing and difficult to achieve, especially when you have trained yourself to do just the opposite.

The third reason shading is less well-known and less frequently used than surface etching and carving is that the technique is comparatively unforgiving. It's easy to make mistakes with shading—and difficult or impossible to correct them. With carving or surface etching, if you blast a second or two too long on any given part of a design, you won't ruin it. However, with the shading technique, you can ruin a project practically in the blink of an eye. Because shading is so unforgiving, and because it takes a bit of practice to achieve the nec-

Norm Dobbins, demonstration piece showing shading on two colors of flashed antique glass (blue over clear and purple over clear), 5" x 3". Partial removal of the flashed layer produces varying tones of the flash color.

Frank Howard, *Rain Forest*, 24" x 60" tempered door panel, design created exclusively with the shading technique.

Glass for Shading

Since shaded etching only affects the surface of the glass, there is no minimum thickness for glass used with the technique. The thinnest crystal wine glasses can be shaded, as can heavy plate tabletops. And because the blasting pressure used with shading is very low, it's the safest technique to use on tempered glass.

Certain types of glass—including flashed glass, mirror, iridized glass and opaque glass—require special consideration when shaded. Flashed glass is most often surface etched, resulting in a nice two-color design (see Chapter 2). However, it can produce much more striking results when shaded. By removing selected areas of the top color layer, the artist can produce innumerable variations of the combined colors.

The subtle tone change that is so attractive in shading can be very effective on the front of a piece of mirror, but disappointing on the back surface, where the effect is more like a faulty mirror than a deliberate design. A similar problem occurs with iridized glass.

Since successful shading depends on the unetched glass appearing dark, shading on dark glass can be very effective. The etching will not show up as well with light coming through the glass from the back as with light reflecting from the front, so it's best if the colored glass is opaque. If not, display the finished piece on a wall or framed with an opaque background.

Resists for Shading

The function of resist is to protect the glass by withstanding the wear and tear of the abrasive and the heat generated by blasting. Compared to carving and surface etching, shading requires both low

Margaret Oldman, *Tattoo Lady*, neon-illuminated panel, 32" x 23". Most parts of the body are carved, while the hair, the gown and much of the tattoo are shaded.

Tohru Okamura, glass platter. The landscape is shaded to emphasize the depth of the vista, while the carved fish swim in the foreground.

It's fairly common to find shading designs that use only variable-area shading, or variable in combination with uniform. Rarely do you find a design that features only uniform-area shading. Many different styles and effects can be created with these two types of shading, and because so many variations are possible, overall design considerations for shading are much more complex than they are with surface etching or carving. You'll need to understand these considerations to take full advantage of the technique.

pressure and short blasting time. For this reason, just about any sheet resist can be used; base your choice on cutting ease and price. As mentioned before, the thicker rubber and soft vinyl resists used for carving are easy to cut, but comparatively expensive and unsuitable for fine detail. Hard vinyl resists are just the opposite.

Found resists can be used for special effects in shading. Try painting or stippling a mixture of two parts white glue and one part water onto the glass surface. When dried and blasted, this resist gives a unique mottled or streaked effect that can look very much like tree bark, moss or mist. The brush strokes you use to apply the glue will show in the finished piece, so an etching created or augmented with this kind of liquid resist will have a painterly look.

Shading Styles

As with carving, the shading technique involves two distinct aspects. The first—numbering elements for the proper sequence of peeling and blasting—requires a good understanding of design principles for

shaded etchings. You also need to know the correct blasting techniques to create the effects you want. However, both the rationale for numbering and the blasting techniques are very different for shading than for carving.

There are two basic types of shading. In *uniform-area* shading, the entire element is shaded to a uniform value of gray. It's not easy to create the same value throughout an element: pausing while blasting, or changing the blasting speed for just a fraction of a second, can cause a disruption in an otherwise uniform area. In *variable-area* shading, the degree of shading varies from light to dark within a single element.

UNDERSTANDING DESIGN FOR SHADING

Since shading is a multistage technique, you'll need to begin with a line drawing; in fact, the same line drawings used for carving can be used for shading. However, in addition to your original design, you'll also need a shaded or rendered version of the design. The reason for this is that the analysis for stage-numbering is based on the comparative shades of gray within elements. Since a line drawing does not have shades of gray, you have to add them by shading the design on paper as you want it to look on glass. Each element must be shaded, both to provide a distinct shade of gray on either side of a common edge, and to realistically represent

Uniform-area shading.

Variable-area shading.

the design. Only after the design is shaded can you analyze it for the proper blasting sequence.

Even if you have no art training, you shouldn't hesitate to start this process. Using your best guess about comparative tones, just go through your pattern, shading each element to a different gray at the point where it touches another element. Number your pattern based on this shaded drawing, then go ahead and blast your glass. After shading a few patterns, you'll be more comfortable with the process and can focus on improving the realism of your shaded designs.

To better understand where the light and dark tones should be, find a photo in a book or magazine (or take a photo yourself) of the subject of your design. If the photo is in color, convert it to a gray-scale image by making a black-and-white photocopy. Enlarge the image to the correct size for your project, then trace over it to produce a line drawing. Unless your black-and-white photocopy has the same shading you want in your etching, you'll need a second copy of the line drawing. Shade one, using the black-and-white photo or photocopy as a guide for placing gray tones; this will be your guide for analyzing and numbering. The second will be used for cutting your resist. (This technique is also useful for creating a line design for carving; you just won't need the gray-scale image for numbering.)

If you have no photo of your subject, try to shade in the light and dark areas of your pattern where they logically should be. When shading a drawing of a flower, for example, the lower petals are generally darker than the upper petals at the places where they touch, since they are in shadow. If your subject is a killer whale, you have to shade the upper

(continued on page 104)

The color photo of a flower has been enlarged in black and white with a photocopier (top). The traced image (right) is numbered for etching, based on the shaded line drawing (left). If the gray shades show up well on the photocopy, you won't need to make a shaded drawing—unless you want to change the shading.

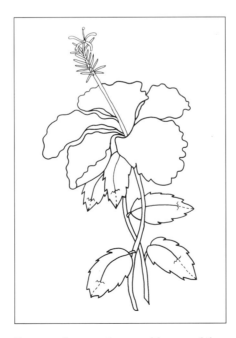

The same flower pattern used for one of the carving projects in Chapter 6. A line drawing like this can be used to mark resist for a shaded etching. Note that the dotted line extensions and zigzags used for disappearing lines have already been added.

A shaded version of the drawing. This is needed before the line drawing can be numbered for the blasting sequence.

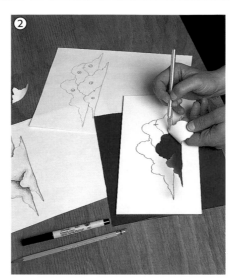

Because two of the three clouds in this project are separated by disappearing lines, there are a total of five elements. As with carving, the disappearing lines are handled by artificially dividing the element along an extension of the line. Blast the area around the artificial cut line only when the second half of the element is blasted, not the first. Thus, the etched line disappears on the glass just where it disappears on the pattern.

1 With the resist on the glass and the design cut, remove the #1 element in preparation for etching. Keep the shaded pattern with you while you blast so you can see the shading you are trying to duplicate on the glass.

2 When the #1 element is blasted, remove the resist from the #2 element and blast. Note the disappearing line.

3 Blast the #2 element. As you approach the previously blasted edge of the #1 element, move the nozzle a bit faster or pull it back a bit. That way you won't ruin the definition between #2 and #1 by overblasting. Note how easily you can see the shading by holding the glass slightly in front of the light, with the back of the cabinet in shadow.

4 Continue to remove resist and blast, etching each element in its correct stage and to the degree indicated on the shaded pattern.

5 The finished piece.

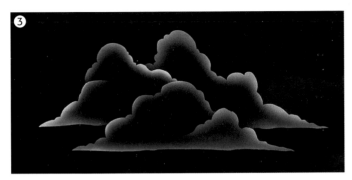

Because shading is such a flexible technique, the same design can be shaded in many ways. Here are a few possibilities. Numbers 1 through 4 use the same numbering sequence; only the type of shading varies. As it happens, the numbering sequence would be the same if the elements were carved—but this is not always the case with shaded designs. Number 5 is a case in point. The same design has been shaded differently, and as a result, the numbering sequence is completely changed.

1 These clouds are almost all white against a clear, dark background, with only a little dark area showing where they touch. The clouds in front are slightly lighter where they touch those in back, and so are blasted first. There is low contrast within each cloud and low contrast between clouds. The transition zones from light to dark are relatively narrow and are concentrated where the clouds touch.

2 In this rendering, the clouds are darker overall. There is fairly high contrast, both within each cloud and between the clouds. The transition zone is much wider here, spreading almost all the way across each cloud.

3 These clouds are almost all dark, but have narrow white edges to separate them from each other. There is medium contrast within and between the clouds, and the transition zone is very narrow.

4 In this piece, the background has been etched completely white, so the edges of the clouds that touch the background have to be darker to show up against it. In other respects the shading is very similar in number 2.

5 In this rendering, the top of each cloud is darker than the bottom part of the same cloud, so clouds in back are lighter where they touch clouds in front. This changes the numbering sequence completely; otherwise, the shading is similar to number 1.

Art Glass Environments, *Toto*, tempered plate glass door panel, multistage shaded design, 23" x 79" x ¼", design: Nancy Rich; etching: David Rakszawski.

Bonnie Brown, insulated window, 4' x 5', photo: Ken Altshuler. Surface etching in the vase and lower background obstructs the view, while narrow outlines define the vase and lower flowers. Variable-area shading results in delicate, realistic flowers and foliage.

part of the body darker than the lower part because that's the natural color of the animal.

These examples illustrate the two primary reasons why certain elements are lighter or darker than others: (1) lighting, and (2) the natural color of the subject. Although it's easier to understand and control these variables—especially at first—by working from photos, a basic drawing or airbrushing class is also a great help.

A key concept in shading is the basic difference between shading *within* elements and shading *between* elements. Shading between elements must vary abruptly to sharply define the edges of the elements. Variations are controlled by the sequence of removing resist and blasting. The artist controls

this by defining the shading on paper and determining a sequence of blasting that will produce the same shading on glass. The contrast level can be as high as 100 percent (one element black and the other white where they touch) or as low as 5 to 10 percent (one element medium gray and the other medium light gray where they touch).

Shading within the perimeter of the element varies from light to dark gradually, without distinct edges, and shows the contour of the element. Variations in shading within an element are created freehand by the artist, by blasting more or less heavily within different areas of the element. Within each element, the shading can vary depending on how much of the area is light or dark, where the transi-

tion from light to dark starts in the element, and how wide the area of transition is.

Shading Your Design on Paper

The best way to shade your design is with a sharpened pencil, using the side of the lead to cover a relatively large area within an element. Covering a large area makes it easier to produce an even gradation between light and dark, resulting in a more realistic effect. Start at the edge of an element where you want a darker tone, and work toward the opposite edge, using less and less pressure as you get closer to the area you want to be lighter. Go back over the element several times if necessary to get the gradation from dark to light the way you want it. Then go on to the

Barry Hood, *Winter Walk* (detail), door panels 116" x 85" overall, photo: Roger Wade. The trees in this shaded winter landscape are reverse shaded, showing up as dark against the white snow. Notice the effective use of the dark (very lightly shaded) areas as the tree shadows.

produces a light color on a dark background. If you confuse the two, you may blast areas that were shaded with the pencil, creating light shades where dark should be.

It's also important to understand—especially as you learn the shading technique—that shading on glass can't be as sensitive and delicate as shading on paper. The finest blast nozzle produces a line 30 or 40 times wider than a pencil point, and with less control. In addition, once an area of glass is shaded, it can't be erased. For these reasons, you shouldn't labor to make your pencil drawing perfectly realistic; your blaster probably won't be able to duplicate it.

The Stage-Numbering Process

When you've shaded all elements in your design, you can proceed with analyzing the blasting sequence. Numbering a shaded design is very similar to numbering a design for carving, except instead of analyzing for the sequence of overlap, you analyze for the sequence of light and dark. In carving, an element that is on top of another is carved first. In shading, an element that is lighter than another where they touch is blasted first, *whether or not it is on top of its neighbor.*

In the drawing at the top of page 106, all elements are shaded. Each has been assigned a letter for the purpose of this exercise.

1 Focus your attention on any element. Let's start with C. Ask: *What other elements does this element touch?* One touching element is A.

2 Ask: *Which one of these elements is lighter along the edge where they touch?* A is lighter.

3 Move the focus of your attention to A, the element that is lighter along the edge.

next element and do the same, and so on until all the elements are shaded. Remember your goals: first, to make sure every line separating elements has a darker shade on one side than the other; and second, to create a design that's as realistic as possible.

If you have two elements that should both be dark (or light) where they touch, just make sure that one is slightly darker than the other. If they are the same shade, their edges will not show, and they will be impossible to number.

Common Problems in Shading Designs
People learning to shade sometimes confuse the processes of applying pencil to paper with that of applying abrasive to glass. Although in both cases you're affecting color, the visual results are opposite. Pencil on paper yields a dark color on a light background, while blasting abrasive onto glass

This drawing has been shaded to determine the blasting sequence.

Ellen Abbott and Marc Leva, *Dolphins*, interior wall in a reception room, 5' x 7'. The dolphins are carved, while the fluid quality of the water is represented by shading over cut resist. The misty area around the dolphins' upper bodies is created by freehand shading.

One at a time, consider the other elements that touch A. For each of these, ask: *Which element is lighter along the edge where the two elements touch?* Keep your focus on the element which is lighter along the common border.

4 Repeat this process until you reach an element that is lighter than all the other elements it touches. Here, D fits the criteria and becomes a #1 element.

5 Now return to the unnumbered elements. Repeat steps 1–3 until you find another element that is lighter along its common edges than all *unnumbered* elements it touches. Assign the element a number that is one number higher than the highest element it touches. If it does not touch any other numbered elements, it will be another #1.

6 Repeat the process until all elements are numbered. Look below to see the correct numbering sequence for this shaded illustration.

The Blasting Process

Blasting a complex shaded design requires the kind of control that only comes from practice, with careful attention to the physical setup of equipment and hand motions. Shading can be done equally well with a pressure or siphon system. Some artists absolutely swear by one system (and swear *at* the other), while others feel the opposite. This extreme difference of opinion seems to be caused by poor understanding of the equipment or by the frustration of using equipment that is set up improperly for glass etching (see Chapter 8).

USING A PRESSURE SYSTEM

Shading requires very little blasting pressure; in fact, it should be just barely enough to etch the glass with each pass of the nozzle. This will be somewhere between a half pound and five pounds per square inch with a pressure blaster, and it probably won't even register on your pressure gauge.

Regulators are not high-precision equipment, and adjusting the pressure is a little tricky. Always start with your blaster unpressurized. Hold the stopper up (in the

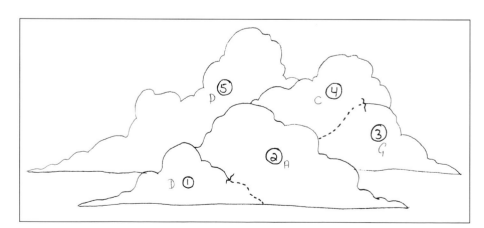

The numbered line drawing. The numbering sequence happens to be identical to the sequence that would be used for a carved version of this design; this is not always the case.

closed position) and slowly adjust the regulator until you hear a slow, steady stream of air going into the blaster. This should be enough to pressurize the blaster and hold the stopper in place. Adjust the abrasive to a steady, light flow. If your blaster has a screw lock stopper, start with the lowest pressure that will still etch the glass with the nozzle about 6" away.

Now test the pressure on a piece of scrap glass, moving the nozzle at medium speed (about 2" to 3" per second) with the nozzle about 6" from the glass. The stripe of the etch on the surface of the glass should be no more than about 40 to 50 percent gray, and $1/2$" to $3/4$" wide. If you get a solid white etch, move your hand more quickly, lower the pressure, or increase the distance from the nozzle to the glass. If the gauge is not registering, you'll have to adjust the pressure by turning the regulator handle by $1/4$ and $1/8$ turns.

Heather Matthews, *Obi Fire Screen*, tempered clear plate glass, reverse surface-etched (white) background with light shading in the ribbon shapes, 33" x 36" x $3/8$", photo: Tim Matthews.

USING A SIPHON SYSTEM

Shading is the only abrasive etching technique where a siphon system can be as effective as a pressure system—if you have the right type of siphon system. Some have a trigger on the gun that is either all the way on or all the way off,

Art Glass Environments, tempered plate glass door panel (detail), overall size 18" x 70" x $1/4$", design: Nancy Rich; etching: David Rakszawski

with no in-between. Others are adjustable: the more you pull the trigger, the more air you get and vice versa. The adjustable type is best for shading, since it offers pinpoint on-off control, as well as precise control of the etch density.

With this type of siphon system, experienced glass etchers can start out with almost any pressure and successfully throttle the flow to the right amount with the trigger. When learning the process, set the regulator at about 40 psi to avoid overblasting if your trigger finger slips. Practice on scrap glass until you develop a feel for the trigger and the distance from the glass that gives you the best control.

BLASTING THE #1 ELEMENTS

The following instructions are very general. Keep in mind that the actual number of passes across or around an element will depend on the size of the element, how much of it you want to etch and how wide or narrow the gradation zone is. Your design may call for certain elements to be mostly dark (unetched) with only a little halo of white at the edge—or the reverse. The contrast in touching elements can be high or low, depending on how much you etch the respective elements. The important thing to know is that you control all of these variables.

When your blaster is properly adjusted and the resist is peeled from all #1 elements, you're ready to blast. Because these are #1 elements, the edges (or portions of the edges) will be blasted to white.

Move the nozzle around the portion of each element to be etched, parallel to the edge of the resist. With the first pass, point the nozzle at the resist—not the glass— about $1/4$" from the edge of the exposed glass. Move the nozzle about

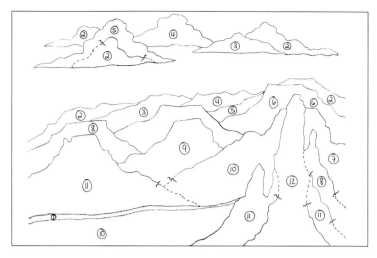

Above left: The shaded line drawing for the project shown on the opposite page. The premise underlying this particular shading is that the rock spires and mesas are made of dark volcanic rock, and that an afternoon haze makes the distant mesas appear increasingly light. The edges of the clouds are dark against the bright sky. Above right: The numbered line drawing.

2" to 3" per second, and allow only the overspray to spill onto the glass. This will create a very light etch (between 20 and 40 percent density) at the edge of the element.

With the second pass, work a little faster and point the center of the abrasive spray at the edge of the resist. With the third pass, increase the speed again, or hold the nozzle further from the glass. Point the abrasive spray directly at the glass this time, about $^1/_4$" to $^1/_2$" in from the edge of the resist.

By increasing the speed with which you move the nozzle (or its distance from the glass surface) as you move away from the edge of the resist and inward toward the center of the element, you create a gradually diminishing density of etch. This means the edges of the element will be whiter and the center darker, with a nice, even gradation between. Complete one element at a time before moving on to other elements with the same number.

STAGE TWO AND BEYOND

Now peel off the #2 elements. Each of these will have resist around its

perimeter where it touches higher-numbered elements, and no resist where it touches #1 elements. Along any edge where a #2 touches a #1, the #1 will be relatively light in color and the unblasted #2 will be very dark. Now you can clearly see why elements with lighter edges in your shaded design are peeled first in the sequence.

Start blasting the #2 elements only where there is resist at the perimeter (i.e., where they touch higher-numbered elements). Don't start where they touch #1 elements; since there is no longer protective resist on the #1's, you could quickly obliterate the distinction between the elements. This can happen in a split second when working with small elements or if your hand gets a little too close. Whenever you approach the edge of an element that has already been blasted, move the nozzle a little faster or pull it back from the glass to lessen the etch density. Move the nozzle in the same pattern as when blasting #1 elements.

Continue blasting the remaining stages until all elements are shaded according to your pattern. As a rule of thumb, blast lightly

with the first few passes. You can always blast more if desirable—but you can never 'erase' shading that's too dense.

The Importance of Lighting

Good lighting in your blasting cabinet is critically important for successful shading. Here are some suggestions to supplement the lighting guidelines in Chapter 8.

It's important when shading to have a dark background in the cabinet; that way, even a light etch will be visible if well lit. This can be achieved in various ways. One solution is to tape a black garbage bag to the back wall of your cabinet. Another simple answer is to spray paint the background black. If you don't wish to have a permanent black background, you can also paint a piece of masonite or plywood black and position it in the cabinet against the far wall. All of these solutions require constant maintenance; they become coated with light-colored dust, and blasting causes the paint to erode.

With adjustable lighting, you can simply point the light forward,

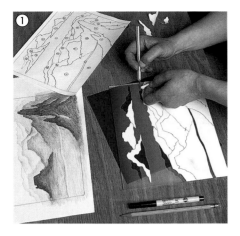

1 The sky in this landscape design is light and hazy in contrast to the elements that touch it, so it is blasted first. Here, the #2 elements are removed.

2 Continue removing resist and blasting elements according to the numbered sequence.

3 The finished piece. Because paper is opaque and glass translucent, the images will never look quite the same. Also, as you see how the image develops during blasting, you may want to make changes in the shading. Since the glass was shaded on the second surface, the image appears reversed.

allowing the back of the cabinet to be in shadow. This will give a very effective dark background. Fluorescent lighting is not good for shading. Since it illuminates the back of the cabinet as brightly as the front, the shading will not show up well.

Your light source should also be positioned either low in the cabinet, pointing up, or high in the cabinet, pointing down. Ideally, it should be on the left side of the cabinet if you are right-handed, and vice versa if you're a lefty. With this positioning, you won't

have to stare straight into the bulb while working, and your etched surface will be strongly illuminated. Shading does not allow for misjudgement. If your lighting is poor, you'll almost always overblast your projects. This can happen quickly, and can ruin a project before you realize it.

Practice ... and Enjoy

When you have achieved some success in shading, you'll undoubtably want to experiment with combining carving and shading. Start with simple designs and combinations that use shading in background areas and areas that will highlight the carving. When combining abrasive-etching techniques, always do the carving first, then any surface-etched areas, then the shaded areas—each in its own numbered sequence. This will keep the high pressure and heavy blasting of the other techniques from ruining the shaded areas.

Although shading is a little tricky to learn, it's an incredibly satisfying process. Neither carving nor surface etching offers the delicacy and range of expression of shading. Don't be shy about getting scrap glass from a local supplier. You'll need lots to practice with, and through practice you'll not only hone your skills, but also find plenty of ideas for future projects.

8

Equipment

The equipment needed for abrasive etching is not particularly complex or expensive; you can purchase what you need, or rent it from a stained glass supplier or equipment rental company. Rental prices are usually reasonable, especially considering how much etching you can do in a short time. To make your rental most economical, have several etching projects ready to work on.

When you do decide to purchase equipment, take time for research. The equipment you'll need will depend in large part on the projects you plan to make. There's no advantage to being over-equipped (and broke) or under-equipped (and thereby unable to pursue the kinds of work you'd like to do).

This chapter covers the basic equipment used for abrasive glass etching: blaster, air compressor, blasting cabinet or blast room with vacuum exhaust, and abrasives. The air compressor provides pressurized air, which is the source of power for the blaster. The blaster takes the compressed air, mixes in abrasive, and directs the resulting mixture at the surface of the glass. The blasting cabinet or blast room provides an enclosed, well-lit environment in which to blast; it also contains the abrasive and the dust generated while blasting.

THE TWO TYPES OF ABRASIVE BLASTERS

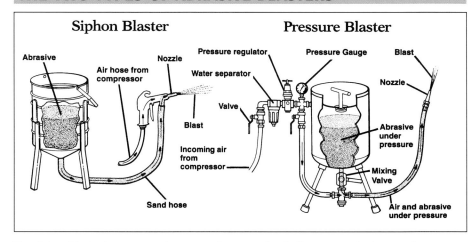

The siphon blaster has an open hopper and a somewhat bulky gun attached to two hoses. There is no abrasive adjustment. The pressure blaster has a welded steel pressurized hopper. The mixing valve is used to adjust abrasive flow, and a single hose carries air and abrasive to a small nozzle. Illustration courtesy of Glastar Corporation.

Blasters and Compressors

The single best decision you can make when buying equipment is to buy from a company that specializes in blasting equipment specifically for glass etching. It will cost less than industrial gear, but more than discount equipment—and be worth every penny. Discount equipment has generally been stripped of all accessories; when you add back all the extras needed to use these models with glass, you end up paying more in the long run.

Two characteristics of compressed air are important in the discussion of blasters and compressors. These are the *pressure* of the air, measured in pounds per square inch (psi), and the *volume* of the air, measured in cubic feet per minute (cfm). The compressor produces the air and the blaster consumes it. The compressor must produce at least as much air as the blaster uses, or it will run out of air and overheat. To match these two pieces of equipment, check the spec sheets for each machine.

As you shop for compressors, you'll generally see two measurements for cubic feet per minute. *Free-air cfm* is not important in

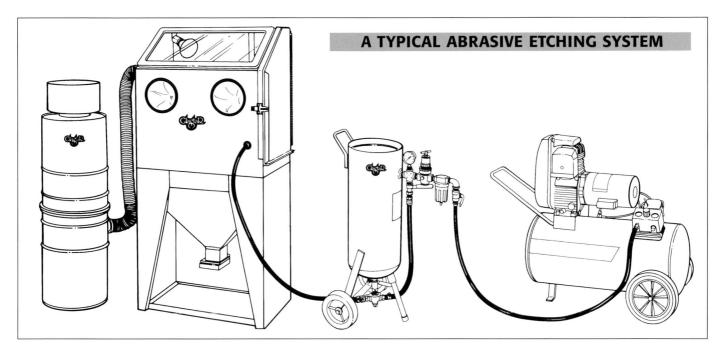

The blasting cabinet and vacuum system provide a well lit environment, while minimizing contamination of your workshop with blasting dust. It's important to match the cabinet with the vacuum (and both items with the size and type of work you'll do).

A blaster—like the pressure blaster shown here—is the heart of the system. It's powered by compressed air; the type and size of blaster determines what size compressor you must use and how fast you can complete a given job.

The compressor runs on electricity or gasoline. Its air production should be matched to the air consumption of the blaster. An air compressor can be used to power many tools besides a blaster. Illustration courtesy of Glastar Corporation.

choosing a compressor for etching, but *standard cubic feet per minute* (scfm) is. The specifications are usually stated as something like "Compressor output: 9 scfm at 125 psi," however—in this book and elsewhere—the term is usually shortened to simply 'cfm.'

Air pressure affects both the speed of your etching and the control you have over special effects. Sufficient air volume is critical to maintain correct pressure. Because they are directly related, volume is always mentioned in conjunction with pressure: e.g., "Blaster air requirement: 7 cfm at 90 psi." At a higher pressure, a given amount of air occupies a smaller space; thus, one cubic foot of air at 20 psi takes up less space at 40 psi. For this reason, it's meaningless to specify a certain number of cubic feet of air unless you know what the pressure of the air is.

THE SIPHON BLASTER

A siphon blaster consists of a blasting gun (a pistol-shaped handpiece with a trigger mechanism or foot pedal), an open hopper of sheet metal or plastic to hold the abrasive, an abrasive hose connecting the hopper to the gun, and an air hose connecting the compressor to the base of the gun. The blaster can be a stand-alone unit, or the siphon gun can be built into a blasting cabinet, with the hopper of the cabinet used as the feed hopper for the gun.

To blast with a siphon system, you fill the hopper with abrasive, adjust the air pressure from the compressor, and pull the trigger (or step on the foot pedal). Compressed air will rush through the gun and out the nozzle. As it does, it passes over the inlet of the abrasive hose, picks up (or siphons)

particles of abrasive, and propels them through the nozzle.

THE PRESSURE BLASTER

The pressure blaster is the choice of most glass-etching professionals, especially for surface etching or carving. It consists of a pressurized hopper of welded steel, a pressure regulator, a water separator, a heavy-duty abrasive hose (which carries the abrasive-and-air mixture from the tank to the nozzle), and the nozzle itself. The on-off switch should be an *air-actuated* foot pedal, which is easier to use than a mechanically actuated pedal. The blaster should be supplied with a small hose and nozzle; avoid the large, heavy ones found with most pressure blasters.

With a pressure blaster, the abrasive is fed into the air stream under pressure. This is a much

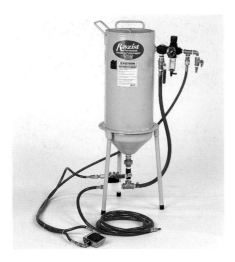

Standard pressure blaster with foot pedal, 100 lb. capacity. Photo courtesy of Rayzist.

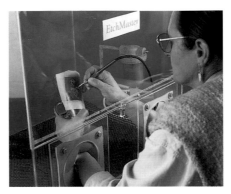

A pencil pressure blaster allows you to etch small stencils on glassware; you can also write or draw directly on the glass without using resist. Photo courtesy of EtchMaster.

more even and efficient method than the siphon system. The increased efficiency allows you to blast more quickly, at a lower pressure and with a smaller nozzle, while using much less air from the compressor. As a result, there is less wear and tear on the compressor and lower maintenance cost. The pressure system also gives you the ability to regulate the exact flow of abrasive from very light to very heavy, independent of the air pressure. This enables you to adjust your blaster for exactly the effect you want.

SPECIALIZED BLASTERS

Miniature blasters, also called *micro* or *pencil* blasters, have a pencil-sized stylus instead of a gun. The nozzle is very small and can be used to etch tiny designs on small pieces of glass, such as crystal jewelry. These typically use much less air than the standard size guns and etch a much smaller area; with the tip of the nozzle against the glass, the zone of overspray at the edge of a blasted line is small enough to render a crisp line without resist. Miniature pressure blasters are faster and more powerful than

miniature siphon blasters. There are even rectangular tips available for these blasters that allow you to etch calligraphy on glass. A word of warning: with micro pressure blasters, as with most other equipment, you get what you pay for.

The *on-site* blaster combines a vacuum return system with a siphon blaster and is designed to be used on glass that is already installed and can't be easily removed. Because the vacuum system sucks up the dust and abrasive as the glass is being etched, the person doing the etching can go into a home or business and work without getting abrasive and dust all over the room. On-site blasters can be used for surface etching and light carving, but not for shading, since the vacuum brush prevents you from seeing the glass while blasting.

AIR COMPRESSORS

An air compressor is made of three parts: the motor runs the air pump, the air pump compresses the air, and the air tank stores the compressed air until it is needed.

The type of compressor usually used for etching glass is electric,

with a two- to five-horsepower motor that operates on 115- or 230-volt electricity. The compressor pump can be either single stage, with a maximum pressure of 125 psi, or two stage, with a maximum pressure of 175 psi. The air tank can hold from 15 to 120 gallons.

Smaller, less expensive compressors are usually mounted on wheels and can be easily moved. More expensive compressors usually have larger air tanks and are not portable. Gas or diesel compressors are available, but they are comparatively noisy, inefficient and expensive—and they emit noxious fumes, as well.

Most people are familiar with horsepower as a measure of compressor size. While this is valuable information, don't decide to buy a compressor based solely on horsepower. It's more important to consider the volume of air produced, and whether it's enough for your blaster, keeping in mind that the air volume produced by a compressor changes depending upon the air pressure. Without sufficient air volume, the compressor will run out of air every few minutes, and you'll have to stop blasting until it builds up pressure again. After a few blast-and-wait cycles, the compressor will be overheated and you'll have to stop blasting until it cools down, or risk damaging it.

Compressor Quality

It's also important to consider the quality of a compressor, unofficially designated as 'consumer,' 'commercial,' or 'industrial.' An industrial-quality 5-hp compressor puts out about twice the cfm of air produced by a consumer-quality 5-hp compressor—and costs about twice as much. Better quality compressors also last longer and cost less per year to maintain.

An average consumer-quality 2-hp compressor will produce about

Comparison of Siphon and Pressure Blasters

CHARACTERISTICS	PRESSURE BLASTERS	SIPHON BLASTERS
Etching speed	Blasts a hole in $1/8$" glass in 5 seconds at 40 psi.	Blasts a hole in $1/8$" glass in 20 seconds at 90 psi.
Blasting pressures	Note: These comparisons are for standard-size blasters. Pressures will vary in work situations. For example, you may need to set a pressure blaster to 5 psi when carving a very small area or up to 60 psi for shading a large area.	
Surface etching	30 to 40 psi	80 to 100 psi
Carving	35 to 45 psi	90 to 110 psi
Shading	1 to 5 psi	30 to 40 psi
Average nozzle size for standard blaster	$3/32$" diameter	$3/16$" diameter
Air volume required	5 cfm @ 40 psi	25 to 38 cfm @ 80 psi (depending on size of air jet in gun)
Independent adjustment of abrasive flow?	Yes	No
Specialty models		
Micro size	Yes	Yes
On-site	No	Yes
On-off control	Least expensive models: manual. Higher priced models: foot pedal.	Trigger (or foot pedal if installed in blasting cabinet at factory).
Price for standard size (U.S. dollars, 1998)	100 lb. capacity: $450 to $700 (price depends on parts included).	50 to 75 lb. capacity: $75 to $100.
Advantages	Uses much less air. Quicker etching with lower pressure. Compatible with a smaller compressor. Can set abrasive flow separate from air pressure. Hand piece smaller and easier to use.	Fine for delicate shading if equipped with a throttling trigger mechanism. Faster and easier to use with projects that require very little blasting.
Disadvantages	Higher initial cost. Takes a little longer to learn to use properly.	Abrasive flow tends to surge unevenly, especially with fine abrasive or humid conditions. Uses a lot of air. Requires a relatively large compressor. Etches slowly. Hand piece relatively large and unwieldy.

6 cfm at 100 psi, and about 7 cfm at 50 psi. This would be adequate to operate a small pressure blaster for about 30 minutes at a time, with 30-minute intervals for cooling between blasting sessions. For a siphon system, you would have to move up to a commercial-quality 5-hp compressor to do comparable work.

When either a pressure or a siphon blaster is used over time, the nozzle slowly enlarges. With even a small increase in nozzle diameter, there will be a dramatic increase in air consumption. If you're blasting a lot and using a smaller compressor, you'll have to

The glass in these windows and door could not be easily removed for etching. An on-site blaster was the solution.

Mitch Olson, an apprentice at Professional Glass Consultants, removes elements from a precut resist.

The brush surrounding the blaster nozzle obscures the portion of the design being etched. It's necessary to go over each area several times to get an even etch.

The finished design (Swift residence, Santa Fe, NM).

replace nozzles frequently. This can be avoided by buying a compressor that will produce at least 50 to 100 percent more air than a new nozzle will require.

Choosing a Blasting Cabinet

The third and last major piece of equipment you'll need is a blasting cabinet. The cabinet should have a large window and a full side- or front-opening door so you can load glass as large as the inside of the cabinet. It will also have a pair of arm holes with gloves attached; these allow you to hold your glass and the blast nozzle without blasting your hands, watch or rings. It must also have a strong vacuum exhaust system. Directional, or point-source, lighting (spotlights or regular bulbs in reflectors) is preferable to fluorescent lighting.

The only disadvantage with a blasting cabinet is that it won't hold a piece of glass larger than its interior dimensions. Blasting chambers of 3'W x 2'D x 2½'H are common, but a 4' wide cabinet is more useful. Of course, the day may still come when you want to etch a larg-

Air Requirements — Continuous Use With New Nozzle

Nozzle Size	CFM at 40 PSI	CFM at 80 PSI	Suggested Compressor
¹/₁₆"	2	4	2 hp
³/₃₂"	5	9	3 to 5 hp
¹/₈"	9	17	5 hp
⁵/₃₂"	14	26	7.5 hp
³/₁₆"	20	38	10 hp

Conclusions: Nozzle size and pressure both affect the air consumption of the blaster. Even a small increase in nozzle size dramatically increases the cfm required by the blaster. Standard pressure blasters set up for glass use an average nozzle size of ³/₃₂" and an average of 40 psi. Standard siphon blasters use an average nozzle size of ³/₁₆" and an average pressure of at least 80 psi.

Blasting Environments

TYPE	ADVANTAGES	DISADVANTAGES
Standard blasting cabinet (not customized for glass)	Enclosed space protects against exposure to abrasive and dust.	Size limited to interior dimensions of cabinet. Loading door may be too small. Lighting may be fluorescent.
Standard blasting cabinet (designed for glass)	Same as above. Full-size loading door. Point-source lighting. Cabinet size good for small- to medium-size projects. No more expensive than other sandblasting cabinets.	Size limited to interior dimensions of cabinet.
Pass-through cabinet	Slots in sides and top allow blasting of large flat sheets of glass, as well as smaller pieces.	Somewhat more expensive than a standard-size cabinet of the same interior dimensions.
Do-it-yourself cabinet	Costs somewhat less than commercial cabinets. Can be made exactly the size you want.	Requires considerable time for research, planning and building.
Blast room	Allows blasting any size glass.	Requires considerable time for research, planning and building. Can be expensive. Requires separate air supply and bulky safety gear.
Outdoors	Less expense than other solutions.	Limited by weather, time of day and environmental concerns. Produces hazardous dust. Difficult to recapture and recycle high-quality abrasives. Requires separate air supply and bulky safety gear.

er piece of glass. In that case, you can arrange to have the work done in the blasting room of a professional etching company.

CABINET OPTIONS

The relatively new *pass-through* cabinets also offer a great solution to blasting flat glass larger than the interior dimensions of a blasting cabinet. They have slots in the sides, and larger pass-through cabinets have slots in the top as well. Using these cabinets, you can etch glass as large as 6' x 8' in an interior chamber of only $2\frac{1}{2}$' x 3'.

You can build your own blasting cabinet, but doing so requires considerable research into optimum proportions for the cabinet and hopper, as well as the details of the vacuum and lighting systems. This is an involved and time-consuming process. Unless you have considerable experience in working with wood and metal, we recommend buying a commercial cabinet.

If you blast large pieces of glass regularly, you'll want to build a blasting room. A properly designed room will have a movable easel that will accommodate glass up to 6' x 10', adjustable lighting for both the front and back of the glass, and a floor that is easily cleaned of abrasive. The room must be well sealed and outfitted with a powerful vacuum exhaust system. A blasting room is not inexpensive, but it's very nice to have. To use it, you must have the proper safety

A pass-through cabinet like the 'Glasspasser,' shown here, allows a large piece of glass to extend out of the cabinet sides and top through narrow, gasketed slots. Photo courtesy of Glastar.

gear (see "Safety Precautions" later in this chapter).

THE BACKYARD OPTION

You *can* blast without a cabinet or a blast room by taking your glass outdoors, leaning it against the house or garage, and blasting away. While this will do in a pinch, it can be unpleasant in the rain, the snow, or the heat of the summer sun, to say nothing of a blustery wind. If you do want to blast outdoors, be sure to wear full safety gear and cover the wall behind your glass with a large, heavy plastic drop cloth. The same blaster that etches your glass will definitely take the paint off your house or toolshed.

BUYING SMART AT THE START

When you are just starting out, you may want to keep your equipment expense to a minimum. A good first setup might include a small bench-top cabinet with vacuum and siphon blaster. A 2- to 4-hp compressor is adequate to operate this system for about 30 minutes at a time, requiring about 30 minutes to cool between blasting sessions. When you want to move up, the first thing to add would be a pressure blaster with foot pedal. This will allow you to etch much more quickly, at a lower pressure, for longer time periods and with less wear and tear on your compressor.

Renting Equipment

If you really want to minimize your investment, consider renting. You can either rent time on someone else's equipment and use it at their location, or rent the equipment itself and haul it to your own workspace.

A growing number of stained glass shops will rent time on their equipment. They may require you to go through a short orientation course to learn how to use the equipment, and it is not unusual to be charged for this service.

If you choose to rent the equipment and take it to your location, you can easily find compressors and siphon blasters at equipment rental companies listed in the Yellow Pages. It will be much more difficult to find blasting cabinets or pressure blasters for rent. You may find it a good compromise to buy your own cabinet and rent the other pieces. Or you may want to buy both cabinet and pressure blaster, and rent the compressor.

Since most rental sandblasters are used by contractors, they are normally used with very coarse sand. Be sure you clean the blaster very well before adding your own abrasive. Just a few particles of coarse abrasive in your fine abrasive can ruin a nice etching.

Remember when renting equipment to note the air requirements for your blaster and find a compressor able to supply enough air. You'll also need to get your own abrasive in advance, and make sure you have any hoses and adaptors required to connect the blaster and compressor.

Abrasives

Although sand was the original material used for glass etching, it's seldom the best choice. Better, safer choices include garnet, aluminum oxide and silicon carbide.

The most common abrasive particle sizes used for glass etching are 120 to 150 grit for architectural projects and 180 to 220 grit for tabletop and gift items. The higher the number, the finer the grit. Smaller etched images and smaller pieces of glass require finer grit because the work is viewed up close, and the smooth finish created by fine grit is more pleasing.

Safety Precautions

Fortunately, abrasive etching is very safe if you follow a few basic rules. While blasting, you need to protect your eyes and skin from the effects of the abrasive, and

An inexpensive tabletop blasting cabinet with siphon blaster is the least expensive way to get started in abrasive etching.

The same cabinet in an open position. Photos courtesy of EtchMaster.

Abrasives for Blasting

Abrasive	Smallest Grit Size	Hardness (mohs' scale)	Advantages	Disadvantages
Silica sand	60 (brown sand) 90 (white crystal sand)	7	Inexpensive on a per-pound basis.	Expensive on a per-use basis. Inhaling dust can cause silicosis. Because it's the same hardness as glass, it etches slowly. Can only be recycled 3–4 times.
Garnet	100	7.5	Moderately inexpensive on a per-pound basis. Can be recycled 4–8 times before wearing down. Safer than sand.	About the same per-use cost as sand.
Aluminum oxide (brown—least expensive; white and pink—harder, more expensive)	600	9	Hard, tough abrasive with sharp particles. Etches quickly. Expensive on a per-pound basis, but can be recycled 60–80 times.	Generates static electricity, causing dust to cling tenaciously to the glass and increasing the chance of scratching while cleaning. Static electricity also causes irritating shocks.
Silicon carbide (black—most common; green—very expensive, not used for glass)	1200	9.5	Cuts glass most quickly of all abrasives. Produces very little static electricity. Cost per hour comparable to aluminum oxide. It can be recycled almost indefinitely since particles break along crystalline cleavage planes, always leaving sharp corners and edges. Because there is no free silica in the dust, it's much safer to use. Causes a 'flashlight effect' during blasting, illuminating the work surface.	The most expensive abrasive per pound (although not per hour). Because of its extra hardness and sharpness, it wears out nozzles relatively quickly.

Conclusions: The abrasives that are more expensive per pound are actually less expensive to use on a per-hour basis. They also etch more quickly (saving on the cost of labor) and are available in much finer grit sizes, which allow you to do finer, better quality work. The more expensive abrasives are also much safer because of the reduced exposure to free silica. Silicon carbide is preferred by many professional glass artists.

your lungs from dust. If you blast close to a loud dust collector or compressor, you should also protect your ears from prolonged exposure to noise.

A quality blasting cabinet will include an effective dust collection system and built-in gloves; these should provide complete protection while you blast. If you are blasting outdoors or in a blast room, you should always wear a hood designed for abrasive blasting. This will protect your head, face, eyes and neck from reflected particles. To keep the dust and abrasive from saturating your clothes, it is best to wear an inexpensive dust-proof blasting suit. Ear plugs or ear cups designed for hearing protection are available from local safety supply companies.

Although some people prefer blasting without gloves at low pressures, elbow-length mid-weight rubber gloves are recommended to protect your hands and arms, especially if you hold the glass rather than setting it on an easel.

Material Safety Data Sheets (available from abrasive suppliers upon request) classify sand as a much more hazardous material than aluminum oxide or silicon carbide. No matter what abrasive you use, you will be creating some amount of free silica (fine silica dust) from etching the glass. *Protect yourself from breathing this dust; it can harm your lungs.* If you blast outdoors on an occasional basis, always wear a good quality replaceable cartridge respirator designed for fine dust. Even if you use a blasting cabinet, you'll need to wear this kind of respirator when-

The artist must wear an air-supplied hood and protective clothes when working in a blast room.

ever you empty your dust collector, refill your blaster, sweep the floor or do anything else that exposes you to the dust.

If you blast outdoors or work in a blasting room, you'll need an air-supplied hood. This system consists of a blasting hood with a separate air pump connected by a long length of hose. Consult with a safety supply company or abrasive equipment company to find the best equipment for your use.

Above all, use common sense while etching glass. Follow manufacturer's instructions when using equipment or chemicals. Ask for MSD sheets for any materials with which you are not thoroughly familiar, and don't operate equipment if you're tired or unsure about how something works. Handle glass, particularly large sheets, with great care; ask your glass supplier for instructions.

Finally, pay attention to your instincts. If something seems dangerous or wrong, stop to investigate. If there's a problem, fix it before you continue. Remember: it's your health. Take responsibility to protect yourself!

Gallery of Etched Glass

Heather Matthews, *Kelp*, ³⁄₄" carved plate tabletop and glass support structure, custom bronze base, internal lighting, 64" x 28" x 16", photo: Tim Matthews.

Don Young, doors of tempered ½" safety glass, surface etched and shaded with photo resist, Vail, Colorado, Public Library, 6' x 8', photo: Kenneth Hayden.

Ellen Abbott and Marc Leva, *Fall*, freestanding panel, marble base, multistage shaded and carved, 18" x 18".

Joan Irving, *Sunlight Juxtaposed*, glass wall, etched plate glass with applied color, entry rotunda of the San Diego International Airport, 50' x 25'.

Jean-Paul Raymond, *Dialogue en Jaune*, surface etched and carved flashed glass mounted in a steel armature, 55" x 23".

Tohru Okamura,
Star Jewelry,
multistage carved bowl,
13½"Dia x 3¼"H.

Margaret Oldman,
Spiral 11, ©1997,
slumped and carved
glass bowl, 16"Dia.

Margaret Oldman,
Nautilus, ©1997,
slumped, carved and
engraved crystal, 14"Dia.

William LeQuier, *Sentinel Series #22*, blown glass vessel with deep carved relief slumped over 1/2" plate glass and 3/8" black Vitrolite. Base is blasted, acid-etched and diamond-wheel cut. Overall: 29½"L x 17"H x 4½"D, photo: Gerrard Roy.

Michael Glancey, *The Still Point*, blown and plate glass, both heavily carved with copper inlay , 14"H x 18"L x 18"D, photo: Gene Dwiggins.

Warren Carther, *Prairie Boy's Dream*, carved and colored 3/4" glass sculpture with stainless steel, two towers, each 10'W x 35'H, photo: Gerry Kopelow.

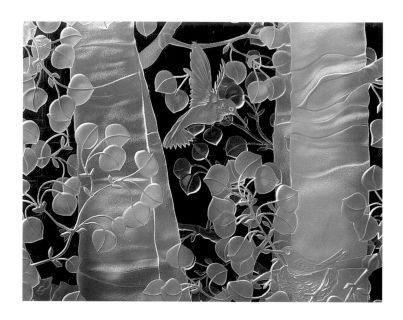

Kathy Bradford, *Faces of the Forest* (details), multi-layered carved wall,
Good Samaritan Hospital, Cardiovascular Institute, Chicago, IL,
21' x 8' x 5", photo: Brian Fritz.

Appendices

Steuben Glass, *St. George Slaying the Dragon*, copper-wheel engraved optical, 8¾"H x 8¼"L, edition of twenty, designer: Donald Pollard, engraver: Charlotte-Linnea Hallett.

Appendix A
Glossary

Abrasive. General name for loose, granular material used to roughen or wear away a substrate. In glass etching this is usually accomplished by exposing the substrate to a high pressure stream of air/abrasive mix.

Abrasive blasting. The correct term for what is often called sand-blasting or sand carving: the process of propelling an abrasive with compressed air to roughen or erode a glass surface. The process is used to produce a frosted texture or to carve and shape the surface.

Acid etching. The process of eroding glass through the use of a chemical that deteriorates and dissolves the glass. The acid used is hydrofluoric acid, a very dangerous chemical.

Air compressor. A mechanical device used to provide high-pressure, condensed air for a variety of tasks. An air compressor is generally composed of three parts: a motor, an air pump, and an air storage tank.

Air intake. A feature of every blasting cabinet or blasting room. Since the vacuum or exhaust system constantly removes air from the enclosed work area, fresh air has to be allowed in to replace it.

Air-supplied hood. A protective head covering used when the person blasting is exposed directly to reflected abrasive particles and dust.

Steuben Glass, Donald Pollard and Linchia Li, *Chinese Sun*, copper-wheel engraving on custom-made crystal glass, 8^1/$_2$"H.

Aluminum oxide. The abrasive most commonly used for etching glass.

Ammonia. An ingredient in some glass cleaners.

Ball valve. A brass or carbon steel valve used on a pressure blaster to regulate air and abrasive flow.

Beveled edge. Refers most com-monly to the treatment of glass edges by grinding and polishing.

Beveling machine. A machine used to grind and polish glass edges.

Black edge. Dark splotches on the back of a mirror, especially at the cut edges or at the edges of etched elements. Black edge can be prevented or retarded by the use of a mirror edge sealant.

Blaster. The cylindrical container which houses the abrasive used in blasting.

Blasting cabinet. An enclosed container used to hold glass while it is being blasted.

Blasting room. A room designed to hold large pieces of flat glass to be blasted.

Bonded glass. Refers to glass pieces which have been adhered together by glue, resin (as in laminated glass), or cement (as in dalle glass blocks).

Borosilicate glass. A specially formulated glass used in laboratory apparatus and equipment as well as applications where it will be exposed to high heat and rapidly changing temperatures. Its low co-efficient of expansion keeps it from shattering under these conditions.

Building codes. National, state and local building codes regulate glass installation in architectural situations.

Cameo. A technique and term borrowed from lapidary work. In cameo cutting, much of the surface layer of the glass object is removed so that the image appears raised in a high bas-relief against the remaining base glass, which is usually of a different color.

Camera-ready artwork. 'Clean,' finished black-and-white artwork used to create a computer-cut or photo stencil. The camera-ready artwork can be a *photo mechanical transfer* (PMT), a film positive, or an image printed by a laser printer or linotronic printer.

Carving. The deep cutting or blasting of glass to produce a three-dimensional design.

Cased glass. Glass consisting of two equally thick layers of different colors.

Ceramic glass. A combination of glass and ceramic; this product is extremely heat resistant.

Cerium oxide. A mild, fine abrasive used in a slurry of water to polish glass.

CFM. Cubic feet per minute. A unit measuring the volume of compressed air delivered by an air compressor per minute, at a given air pressure.

Copper-wheel engraving. This method of cutting glass employs thin copper discs or wheels with edges coated in carborundum or diamond.

Crystal glass. A glass formula containing at least 24 percent lead oxide, which — because of a higher index of refraction — makes the glass softer, clearer and more brilliant than soda lime glass. Also called 'lead crystal.'

Cut glass. A style of glass with a design cut by a stone or copper wheel, leaving a frosted finish in the design. In contrast, brilliant cutting refers to glass with a polished design cut with a stone wheel.

Diatrata glass. An ancient Roman technique. Diatrata takes cameo cutting one step further by undercutting the image so that it is almost free-standing, held to the base vessel by only a few connecting points.

Diamond-point engraving. Engraved images made with a pencil-like instrument with a diamond tip.

Diamond-wheel engraving. Engraving made with stone wheels coated in diamond dust. This method is used for cutting and shaping as well as beveling and polishing.

Dichroic glass. A thin metallic coating on any type of glass; the coating is applied at a high temperature in a vacuum chamber.

Disappearing line. In a multistage carved or shaded design, this is a line that extends into a larger element and disappears before reaching the perimeter of the element.

DSB. An acronym for 'double strength' glass, which is $1/8$" thick window glass.

Edge work. Treatment of the edges of plate glass by cutting, grinding and polishing. Usually applied to glass that is $3/16$" thick or more. Edges can be seamed, ground or beveled in many different configurations.

Engraving. The roughening or eroding of a glass surface by means of scratching either with a diamond-point stylus or with a rotary, impact, wheel or laser engraver.

Etching. Eroding the surface of glass by means of hydrofluoric acid or a weakened bifluoride compound known as etching cream. Through common usage, the term has come to mean abrasive blasting as well.

Film line cutter. A tool that looks like a pencil, but has a sharpened steel loop at the tip.

Fire polishing. Heating a roughened glass surface to a point where it remelts and becomes shiny again—about 1100° to 1200°F, depending on the type of glass.

Flashed glass. A type of flat, stained glass with a thicker layer of clear or light-colored glass and a thin 'flashed' layer of darker colored glass.

Float glass. Flat plate glass made by the float process. The molten glass glides onto a liquid bath of tin alloy, 'floating' on the molten tin to achieve a consistent thickness. Float glass is perfectly polished without further treatment.

French embossing. A very complex and dangerous process that employs various acid solutions to achieve multiple levels and tones in acid etching.

Full lead crystal. Glass containing at least 30 percent lead oxide.

Fusing. The melting together of individual glass pieces in a kiln.

Glass blanks. Unetched glass objects of all sorts sold for the purpose of etching.

Glue chipping. A texture created by blasting the surface of the glass and then applying a layer of hide glue. Upon drying, the glue contracts and rips slivers of glass from the surface, creating a pattern that resembles ice crystals frozen on a window pane in winter.

Grit. Refers to the particles of an abrasive; usually used with a number that indicates the relative size of the particles. The larger the number, the smaller the particles. For example, 120 grit abrasive is commonly used to etch architectural-size glass, but 180 or 220 grit (much finer) is required for the fine details on a glass award.

Hopper. Term for both the open abrasive container in a siphon blaster and the cone-shaped bottom half of a blasting cabinet, which funnels the spent abrasive for recycling.

Hydrofluoric acid. The only acid used to erode glass. It is classified as highly toxic. Both the acid itself and the vapors are considered hazardous materials; the storing and disposal of the product is strictly regulated by OSHA.

Iridized glass. Flat or blown glass with a vapor deposit of metal ox-

Kathy Bradford, detail of carved and shaded design on ¼" plate glass. The artist has used liquid resist to produce the realistic textures of the carved tree trunk and the shaded ripples and reflections on the water.

ides on one surface. The iridized layer, which resembles an oil slick, can be blasted through for a two-tone effect.

Jade crystal. A relatively new term, applied to trophy blanks and sculptural blanks made of regular plate glass, which has a green tint at the edge of the glass.

Laminated safety glass. Normally two layers of ⅛" glass laminated together with a plastic liner between them.

Lathe. A motor with a rotating shaft and a spindle to which engraving wheels of copper, diamond or stone can be attached for cutting glass.

Lead crystal. See crystal glass.

Mask. A common term for resist material with a design on it, especially photo stencils.

Media. Another name for abrasives.

Mil. A measure of thickness used to classify resist materials. A mil is one thousandth of an inch.

Moisture filter/trap. See water separator.

MSDS. Material Safety Data Sheet. An information sheet on any specific chemical product detailing the hazards of using the product. By law, the manufacturer must supply you with MSD sheets for its products on your request.

Mohs' scale. A scale, named after the German mineralogist Friedrich Mohs, which indicates relative hardness from one to ten, with one being the softest.

Negative etch. Etching or blasting the background of an image, leaving the image itself clear or unblasted. Also called reverse etch.

NIOSH. National Institute of Occupational Safety & Health. Look for ratings by this institute when purchasing respirators, respirator cartridges and other safety materials to see if the item is adequate for the intended purpose.

Optical crystal. Crystal glass that is usually made with metals other than lead. This type of crystal is equally clear or clearer than lead crystal, and is usually harder. Optical glass is very expensive.

OSHA. Occupational Safety & Health Administration. This entity sets standards for manufacturing processes, and for handling potentially hazardous materials.

Photo stencil, photo resist, photo mask. A family of pre-imaged masking materials, where the image is produced by a photographic process rather than hand cutting.

Plate glass. Any kind of window glass made by the float method. The term is usually applied to glass over ⅛" in thickness.

PMT. Photo mechanical transfer. A process that photographically translates a drawing into a black-

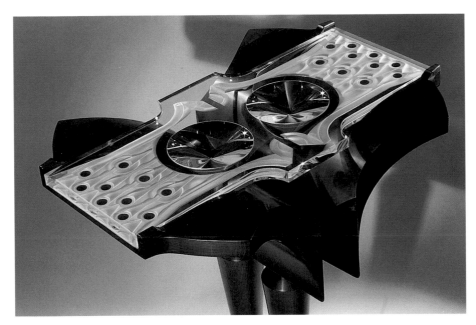

Eric Hilton, *Tidal Pools,* carved heavy-plate tabletop, overall size of table 30" x 24" x 18¼".

and-white image on slick, glossy paper. Used to produce a film positive or to make a photo stencil.

Positive etch. Etching the design elements so that the background is clear and unetched.

Pressure blaster. The most efficient type of blaster.

Pressure gauge. A device that shows the amount of air pressure in an air line or tank.

Pressure regulator. A device that allows the regulation of air pressure.

PSI. Pounds per square inch, a measure of pressure for compressed air.

Resist. Any material applied to the glass to protect it from the etching process.

Respirator. A face mask with cartridges which filter out dust particles; the best are rated by NIOSHA for asbestos, and filter dust particles down to 3 microns.

Reverse etch. See negative etch.

Safety glass. There are two types of safety glass: laminated and tempered.

Sandblasting. Abrasive blasting with silica sand.

Shading. A multistage technique, similar to airbrushing.

Silica sand. A very inefficient abrasive which can cause silicosis if precautions are not taken.

Silicon carbide. Highest quality abrasive for blasting as well as cutting or grinding.

Silicosis. A lung disease caused by prolonged exposure to breathing free silica; large amounts of free silica are created by using sand as an abrasive on glass.

Siphon blaster. The cheapest type of abrasive blaster—also the most common and least efficient.

Slumping. A hot-working technique in which glass is shaped in a kiln with the aid of a mold.

Soda-lime glass. The most common type of glass, made from soda, lime and silica.

Substrate. A term used for any material to be blasted or engraved.

Surface etching. A technique in which all elements are separated by clear spaces and are cut, peeled and blasted at the same time, to the same density.

Squeegee. A spatula-like tool made from a hard but somewhat flexible plastic.

Tempered glass. Plate glass which is rapidly cooled during production, so that the finished glass is under stress. When struck, it breaks into many tiny pieces, thus minimizing injury.

Uniform-area blasting. An area blasted to a consistent density or depth.

Vacuum system. See exhaust system.

Variable-area blasting. In contrast to uniform-area blasting, an area which is carved or shaded to various densities or depths.

Water separator. A device used to remove moisture from compressed air before it reaches your abrasive.

Appendix B
Patterns

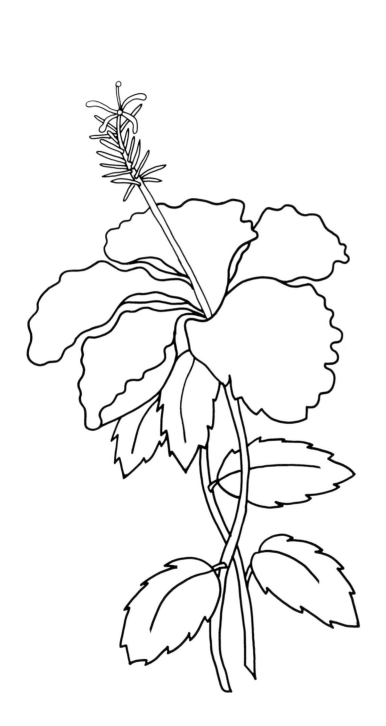

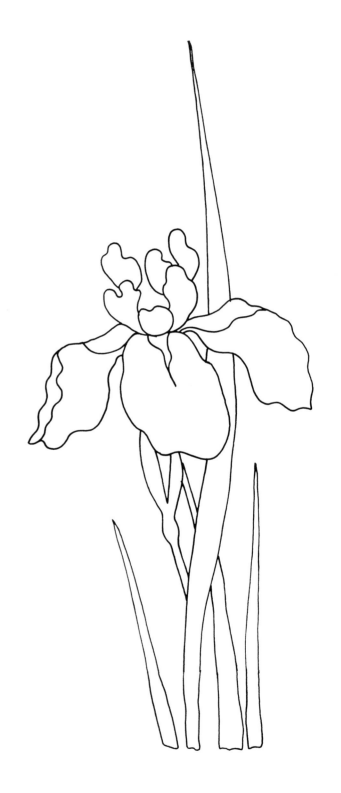

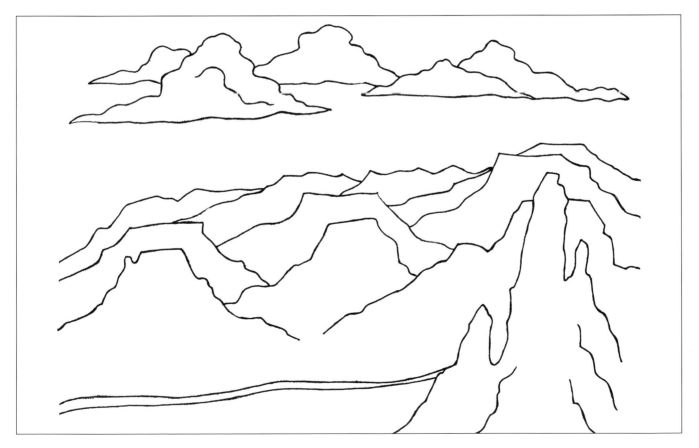

Appendix C
Suppliers

**Professional Glass Consultants /
Etchmasters™**
Norm and Ruth Dobbins
2442 Cerrillos Road, Suite 350
Santa Fe, NM 87505
888-382-4776
505-473-9203
505-473-9218 Fax
www.etchmaster.com
*Through their business, the authors
offer glass-etching books, videos,
seminars, consulting, EtchMaster™
precut stencils (including the patterns
in this book), glass blanks and
equipment.*

GENERAL SUPPLIES:
NORTH AMERICA

Crystal Galleries
1036 North Citrus Avenue
Covina, CA 91722
888-915-6553
626-915-6553
626-915-6193 Fax

Denver Glass Machinery
2800 Shoshone Street
Englewood, CO 80110
303-781-0980

**Econoline Abrasive Products
Division**
Spectra Products Corp.
335 North Griffin
Grand Haven, MI 49417
800-253-9968

Glastar Corporation
20721 Marilla Street
Chatsworth, CA 91311
800-423-5635
818-341-0301
818-998-2078 Fax

John A. Morrison, *Oriental Collage*, carving on ¹/₂" plate glass, metal base, 20"H.

Paragraphics Corporation
1455 West Center Street
Orem, UT 84057
800-624-7415
801-221-1415 Fax

Photobrasive Systems
4832 Grand Avenue
Duluth, MN 55807
800-643-1037
218-628-2002
218-628-2064 Fax

Rayzist Inc.
955 Park Center Drive
Vista, CA 92083
800-729-9478
760-727-8185
760-727-2986 Fax

SCM
W140 N5946 Lilly Road
Menomonee Falls, WI 53051
800-755-0261

Trumans—Skatblast Inc.
7075 State Route 446
Canfield, OH 44406
330-533-3384

General Supplies: Europe

Ebor Glass Equipment Ltd.
James Hill Street
Littleborough, Lancashire OI15
    8AE
England
0706-74411
0706-79950 Fax

**Glasner Sandstrahltechnik
    GMBH & Co. KG**
Gildestrasse 44
4530 Ibbenburen
Germany
05451-45041
05451-45043 Fax

Kansa Craft
The Flour Mill
Wath Road
Elsecar, Barnsley, South Yorkshire
    S74 8HW
England
0226-747424
0226-743712 Fax

TGK—Tiffany Glas Kunst GMBH
Helleforthstrasse 18
33758 Schloss Holte-Stuckenbrock
Germany
05207-1097
05207-50371 Fax

Vitromask Ltd.
Cooks Farm
Stoke St. Michael, North Bath,
    Somerset BA3 5LE
England
01749-840126
01749-840754 Fax

Stencil Materials:
North America

Aicello North America Inc.
800-349-5037 East and Central
800-825-9885 West Coast

Cooper Graphics
156 Thomasmill Road
Holly Springs, NC 27540
800-996-6275

Glass Image
1932 Valley View Lane
Farmers Branch, TX 75234
214-241-3824

Photobrasive Systems
4832 Grand Avenue
Duluth, MN 55807
800-643-1037
218-628-2002
218-628-2064 Fax

Rayzist Inc.
955 Park Center Drive
Vista, CA 92083
800-729-9478
760-727-8185
760-727-2986 Fax

Stencil Materials: Europe

Vitomask Ltd.
Cooks Farm
Stoke St. Michael, North Bath,
    Somerset BA3 5LE
England
01749-840126
01749-840754 Fax

Glass Blanks

Blenko Glass
PO Box 67
Milton, WV 25541
304-743-9081

Dalzell Viking
PO Box 459
New Martinsville, WV 26155
800-237-0005

Durand International
PO Box 5001
Milville, NJ 08332
609-825-5620

Libbey Inc.
PO Box 10060
Toledo, OH 43699
419-325-2100

Schott Glass Technologies Inc.
400 York Avenue
Duryea, PA 18642
717-457-7485

Etching Cream Supplies

Armour Products
PO Box 128
Wyckoff, NJ 07481
201-847-0404

B & B Products Inc.
19721 North 98th Avenue
Peoria, AZ 85382
602-933-2962
602-815-9095 Fax

Appendix D
Reading and Resources

Several worthwhile publications listed below are out of print. You may still be able to find them through a stained glass supplier, used-book shop, or library.

Glass Etching: Surface Techniques And Designs
Norm Dobbins & Debra Felberg Oxley
CKE Publications, Olympia, WA
1988

Glass Etching II: Carving Techniques And Designs
Debra Felberg Oxley & Norm Dobbins
CKE Publications, Olympia, WA
1993

Sand Carving Glass *(out of print)*
L.S. Watson
McGraw-Hill — TAB Books, Blue Ridge Summit, PA
1986

The Encyclopedia of Working With Glass *(out of print)*
Milton K. Berlye
Oceana Publications, Dobbs Ferry, NY
1968

The Techniques of Glass Engraving *(out of print)*
Jonathan Matcham and Peter Dreiser
Larousse & Company, New York, NY
1982

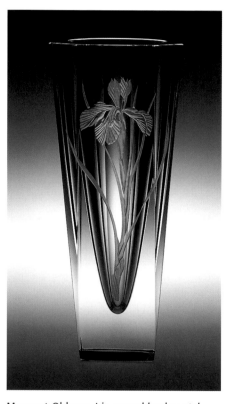

Margaret Oldman, Iris, carved lead crystal vase, 6"H.

Glassforming *(out of print)*
Frederic and Lilli Schuler
Chilton Book Company, Philadelphia, PA
1970

Glass Source Book
Jo Marshall
Collins & Brown, London, England
1990

Glass: A Contemporary Art
Dan Klein
Rizzoli International Publications, New York, NY
1989

New Glass In Europe
Helmut Ricke
Verlagsanstalt Handwerk, Düsseldorf, Germany
1990

Dictionary Of Glass Materials And Techniques
Charles Bray
A&C Black, London, England
University of Pennsylvania Press, Philadelphia, PA
1995

The Artist's Complete Health & Safety Guide
Monona Rossol
Allworth Press, New York, NY
1994

Industrial Pneumatic Technology
Parker Hannifin Corporation, Cleveland, OH
1980

Sandblast Glass Etching
  Video I: Surface Etching Techniques
  Video 2: Multilevel Carving Techniques
  Video 3: Techniques For Shaded Etching
  Video 4: Designing For Glass Etching
Norm Dobbins
Professional Glass Consultants, Santa Fe, NM
1987, 1992

Appendix E
Reference Charts

Mohs' Hardness Scale

This scale is widely used in mineralogy; examples are listed for each classification.

#	
#1	talc
#2	gypsum
#3	calcite
#4	fluorspar
#5	apatite
#6	orthoclase feldspar
#7	quartz
#8	topaz
#9	corundum (alumina, emery)
#10	diamond

Pressure Measurements

POUNDS PER SQUARE INCH	BAR (METRIC UNIT)
14.5 psi	1 bar
30 psi	2.1 bar
50 psi	3.5 bar
60 psi	4.1 bar
72 psi	5 bar
101.5 psi	7 bar
125 psi	8.4 bar
175 psi	12.1 bar

Volume Measurements

CUBIC FEET PER MINUTE	LITERS PER MINUTE
1 cfm	28.3 l/m
5 cfm	141.5 l/m
8 cfm	226.4 l/m
10 cfm	283 l/m
15 cfm	424.5 l/m
20 cfm	566 l/m

Abrasive Grit Sizes

Note:
One micron = 1/1000 mm
Twenty-five microns = 1/1000"

60 grit	254 microns
90 grit	145 microns
120 grit	102 microns
150 grit	89 microns
180 grit	76 microns
220 grit	63 microns
240 grit	50 microns
280 grit	37 microns
320 grit	29 microns
360 grit	23 microns
400 grit	17 microns

* Abrasives finer than 240 grit are considered powders and are called *microgrits*.

Linear Measurement

INCHES	MILLIMETERS
1/16"	1.6 mm
3/32"	2.5 mm
1/8"	3.2 mm
5/32"	3.9 mm
3/16"	4.7 mm
7/32"	5.5 mm
1/4"	6.3 mm
5/16"	7.9 mm
3/8"	9.5 mm
1/2"	12.5 mm
3/4"	19 mm

Appendix F
Contributing Artists and Studios

Ellen Abbott
Custom Etched Glass
Houston, Texas
Pages 5, 15, 40, 69, 97, 106, 121

Melissa Andrews
Savoy Studios
Portland, Oregon
Page 86

Kathy Barnard
Kathy Barnard Studio
Kansas City, Missouri
Pages 7, 79

Brian Baxter
Olynyk/Baxter Collaborative
Vancouver, Ontario, Canada
Page 73

Eric Bergman
Bogata, Columbia
Page 18

Barbara Lillian Boeck
GB Studio
Westwood, New Jersey
Pages 16, 23, 36, 55, 90

Joe Boron
Joey Manic
Capitol Heights, Maryland
Page 70

Kathy Bradford
North Star Art Glass, Inc.
Lyons, Colorado
Pages 128, 132

Bonnie Brown
Etchings
San Rafael, California
Title page, front cover, 35, 57, 61, 104

De Carter-Hoffman
Classical Glass
Costa Mesa, California
Page 92

Warren Carther
Carther Studio Inc.
Winnipeg, Manitoba, Canada
Page 127

Norm and Ruth Dobbins
Santa Fe, New Mexico
Pages 13, 18, 22, 45, 56, 64, 65, 67, 70, 75, 83, 84, 98

J.D. (Jim) Francis
Phoenix Design Studio
Belfair, Washington
Pages 14, 84

Bernice Ferman
Tucson, Arizona
Page 91

Michael Glancy
Glancy Glassworks
Rehoboth, Massachusetts
Pages 89, 126

Goddard & Gibbs Studios
London, England
Pages 70, 71

Deborah Goldhaft
Fire & Ice Glass Studio
Vashon Island, Washington
Page 90

Sue Grauten
Savoy Studios
Portland, Oregon
Page 86

Michael K. Hansen
California Glass Studio
Sacramento, California
Front cover, 27, 31, 34

Eric Hilton
Hilton Glass Studio
Odessa, New York
Pages 20, 42, 52, 56, 87, 133

Barry Hood
Barry Hood Glassworks
Helena, Montana
Back cover, 11, 27, 96, 105

Gordon Huether
Architectural Glass Design
Napa, California
Page 59

Frank Howard
Creative Sandblasting
Plant City, Florida
Page 98

Joan Irving
Joan Irving Glass Design
San Diego, California
Front cover, 9, 26, 62, 71, 77, 122

Kristall-Rimpler
Zwiesel, Germany
Page 10

Rich Lamothe
Savoy Studios
Portland, Oregon
Page 86

Duncan Laurie
Degnan-Laurie Glassworks
Jamestown, Rhode Island
Pages 40, 54

K. William LeQuier
Readsboro, Vermont
Pages 82, 125

Marc Leva
Custom Etched Glass
Houston, Texas
Pages 5, 15, 40, 69, 97, 106, 121

Melissa Malm
Jackson, Wyoming
Front cover, 28, 45, 47

Heather Robyn Matthews
Heather Glass
Soquel, California
Pages 55, 107, 119

Elizabeth Mears
Windy Hill Glassworks
Fairfax Station, Virginia
Pages 21, 31

Julian Mesa
La Mancha Glass Gardens
Tarpon Springs, Florida
Pages 74, 81

Karin Mesa
La Mancha Glass Gardens
Tarpon Springs, Florida
Pages 74, 81

Annie Morningstar
Fresh Northwest Design
Gig Harbor, Washington
Page 29

John Morrison
Cornerstone Glassworks
Dallas, Texas
Pages 30, 32, 38, 57, 138

Nathan Allan Glass Studios
Richmond, British Columbia,
  Canada
Page 85

Rebecca Odom
Blasted Glass
Briarcliff, Texas
Page 30

Tohru Okamura
Yokohama, Japan
Front cover, 27, 43, 54, 100, 124

Margaret Oldman
Illuminations
San Francisco, California
Pages 17, 19, 50, 99, 124, 140

Markian Olynyk
Olynyk/Baxter Collaborative
Vancouver, Ontario, Canada
Page 73

Nina Paladino-Caron
California Glass Studio
Sacramento, California
Front cover, 27, 31, 34

Zoe Pasternack
New York City, New York
Page 28

David Rakszawski
Art Glass Environments
Boca Raton, Florida
Pages 104, 107

Jean Paul Raymond
Glass Studio Cologne
Köln, Germany
Pages 23, 37, 49, 123

Nancy Rich
Art Glass Environments
Boca Raton, Florida
Pages 104, 107

Sandra Cole Rodger
Joey Manic
Capitol Heights, Maryland
Page 70

Ramon Romero
Windsor, Ontario, Canada
Page 8

Barry Sautner
Sautner Cameo Studio
Landsdale, Pennsylvania
Pages 15, 81

Wendy Saxon-Brown
Saugerties, New York
Pages 58, 60, 78

Lucinda Shaw
Acacia Art Glass Studios
Baltimore, Maryland
Page 33

Skyline Design
Charles Rizzo, Mark Stegen
Chicago, Illinois
Page 60

Steuben Glass Inc.
Donald Pollard, Linchia Li,
  Charlotte-Linnea Hallett
New York City, New York
Page 130

Raquel Stolarski-Assael
Mexico City, Mexico
Page 80

David Stone
Kensington Glass Arts Inc.
Kensington, Maryland
Page 19

Laurie Thal
Jackson, Wyoming
Front cover, 28, 45, 47

Char Vowell
Fireworks Glass
Waialua, Hawaii
Page 80

Dan Woodward
Savoy Studios
Portland, Oregon
Page 86

Don Young
Don Young & Associates
Fort Worth, Texas
Pages 16, 29, 120

Wayne "Wally" Zampa
Zampa Design Studio
Paradise, California
Pages 25, 85

Appendix G
Index